Stepping Up

STEPPING UP

*Finding Healing for
Your Life and Hope
for the Future*

DONALYN POWELL

NEW YORK

NASHVILLE • MELBOURNE • VANCOUVER

Stepping Up

Finding Healing for Your Life and Hope for the Future

Published in New York, New York, by Morgan James Publishing. Morgan James is a trademark of Morgan James, LLC. www.MorganJamesPublishing.com

The Morgan James Speakers Group can bring authors to your live event. For more information or to book an event visit The Morgan James Speakers Group at www.TheMorganJamesSpeakersGroup.com.

Unless otherwise indicated, scripture comes from the Holy Bible, New International Version®, NIV® Copyright ©1973, 1978, 1984, 2011 by Biblica, Inc.® Used by permission. All rights reserved worldwide.

Scripture marked TLB is taken from The Living Bible copyright © 1971 by Tyndale House Foundation. Used by permission of Tyndale House Publishers Inc., Carol Stream, Illinois 60188. All rights reserved.

ISBN 9781683503897 paperback
ISBN 9781683503903 eBook
Library of Congress Control Number: 2016920900

Cover Design by:
Kelly Thomlin

Interior Design by:
Chris Treccani
www.3dogdesign.net

In an effort to support local communities, raise awareness and funds, Morgan James Publishing donates a percentage of all book sales for the life of each book to Habitat for Humanity Peninsula and Greater Williamsburg.

Get involved today! Visit
www.MorganJamesBuilds.com

Dedication

To my daughter, Shelley Lynne,

son-in-law, Greg,

and grandson, Jackson Schuster.

I pray you will always embrace your worth in Christ and know He has a purpose for your life that only you can fulfill.

You are my heart.

Love, Nanny/dp

Contents

Foreword

D onalyn lives in the foothills of the Blue Ridge Mountains of Virginia. Her down-to-earth style makes her quite at home with her surroundings.

A desire to serve the Lord led her to seek God's will for her life. As a result, she has served the Lord for many years as a Sunday school teacher and youth counselor because she was drawn to the needs of today's young people. She has worked with teenagers on many levels outside of the church. This has given her the opportunity to understand their problems as *they* see them and has allowed her to share her faith in God. Working with teens who struggle with suicide has given her an insight and ability to reach these young people where they struggle with life.

After completing college with a degree in art, she was recognized as an award-winning photographer and designer. Remembering her desire to serve the Lord, she dedicated her talents and life to Him.

When you meet her, she captures you with a gracious smile radiating from an inner Southern warmth. The energy she possesses flows in your direction, and you are captivated by her presence. But what stands out about her is her love for the Lord.

It's clear she has reached the heart-cry of the young people whose letters, stories, and thoughts appear on the pages of this book.

Linda Beahm, MD
Family Practice

Acknowledgments

Once upon a time there was a young girl who read a book and dreamed of becoming a writer. After she went to college she became an art director and forgot about her dreams of writing. One day she heard Charles Stanley preach a sermon, and she gave her life and talents to the Lord. It wasn't long after this she dreamed she died and went to heaven. The Lord asked her what have you done with everything I gave you?, and she was ashamed of her empty hands. The next day she began putting her first book together, and God sent people in her life to help her, as He has done with this book.

A special thank you to my prayer warriors, Dr. Robert Delong and his wife Janice, along with Lois Daisy and not forgetting my encouraging friends, Debbie Rogers, and Lisa Perry.

To my prayer group and sisters in Christ—Nancy, Jean, Bobbett, Eileen, and Sharon—who have prayed over this book and for everyone who will read these pages. How awesome to know in advance you have been prayed for.

To Amy Collier, the best social media publicist I know. She keeps things running while I write.

To Dr. D. Michael Parker, my husband and educated redneck, who has supported my work for many years.

To Amanda Rooker and her editing team at SplitSeed— they are the best. Thank you!

A special shout out goes to Terry Whalin and Morgan James Publishing, thanks for believing in this book, and I could not get through the process without editor, Megan Malone getting me through the process, a big ole hug your way from me.

To Dr. Linda Beahm, who encouraged the writing of this book and spent many long hours gathering medical facts on teen suicide.

A special thank you to Mark Creasey. Best IT guy I know. Your house calls saved me.

To my church family, my pastor, and his wife, Carl and Debby Weiser. I am so blessed to be a part of Hyland Height Baptist Church, who has encouraged and prayed for me as I continue to grow in the Lord. You are a blessing to me!

To Rob at Photoworks, who turned my photographas around for publication, Thans Rob.

To Wanda Cantor, we share the same love for the Lord. I can't begin to list all that you are to me.

Some of ya'll have been blessed to have awesome moms and Granniess. I'm one of them. My mama and Granny taught me the love of Jesus at a young age. Teaching me the love of Christ has carried me to where I am today. If you are blessed to have a Granny and mama like mine, then I pray you will spend many hours at their side, soaking up all the wisdom they have to impart.

As I finish this manuscript and read over the words, I am reminded of how the Holy Spirit got a hold of me and encouraged me to put this book together. I owe everything to my Lord and Savior—especially the confident assurance to share His promises and His unconditional love. God has a purpose and a plan for your life. Don't miss His blessings!

Donalyn

Preface

His call came late one Sunday night. "Hello, is this Donalyn Powell?"

"Yes, it is."

"I overheard my father talking about you with someone on the plane coming home from Washington, DC. I understand you're writing a book on teen suicide and that you're taking letters from teenagers who have tried to kill themselves. I can't tell you my name. I need to know this is confidential."

I assured him it would be, and he began his story.

It seemed as if he couldn't express what he wanted to say fast enough. I realized immediately he needed someone to just listen to him. Even though his thoughts were all about suicide, deep within him was a driving desire to find someone who could give him a reason to live.

"I tried to kill myself last year, and I just tried to kill myself again, but we can't tell anyone because of the high position my father holds."

I wondered what would happen if he gave his father the chance to understand the pain he was going through. The last words from this young man, whom I could not see, shared the true emptiness of his pain: "I don't even know who I am."

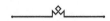

As I entered the room, I found myself looking into the fear-filled eyes of Claire, a beautiful sixteen-year-old girl. She hadn't answered my knock, but I'd entered anyway. At first she wouldn't talk. I could only sit by her and recall her recent past.

Claire had no desire to be part of the world that existed beyond the four walls of her bedroom, but she'd run out of excuses to stay home from school. Others had noticed her withdrawal, but felt it was just a temporary reaction to the recent break-up with her boyfriend Scott. There was much more.

It had been only a year since her parents had fought through a painful divorce. Claire had grown tired of feeling as if she were the only means of communication between them. She was torn by her love for both of them.

She had been friends with Scott for a long time. They'd grown up in the same neighborhood, gone to the same school, and attended the same church. They began dating only weeks after her parents announced they were getting a divorce. His parents had divorced several years earlier, so he was able to understand what she was going through. She turned to him for the attention and affection she didn't feel she was getting at home.

Their relationship progressed physically further than either had expected. Claire knew she was too young to get married, but she had become emotionally and physically dependent on Scott.

When Scott began to feel the pressure of their relationship—and the responsibility for helping her get through her parents' divorce—he unexpectedly announced that they were too young to be so involved.

His short and cold explanation made her feel used and ashamed of being physically involved with him. Her loneliness, guilt, and rejection were more than she could bear.

It was only days ago that she had been forced to leave her room and return to school—and on that same afternoon, she had tried to take her own life. Now, suddenly, she turned and hugged me. Her tears were wet against my shoulder, and in her broken voice she whispered, "I'm so tired of hurting."

Last summer I found myself surrounded by deeply moving stories of young people who had taken their own lives. The first story of suicide left me in shock. When it was followed by another, I wondered and feared who would be next. I could feel the hurt and pain of these victims.

And then there were those close to the victims—in some cases, the wounds never heal. Some feel forever guilty, wondering what they could have done to prevent an unnecessary death.

I tried to put each tragic story out of my thoughts and think of "brighter" things. But each time I did, another hurting youth would find his way into my life. I was overwhelmed. I could understand what each one was feeling, and it forced me to relive the pain of my own past.

When I turned nineteen, I began an eight-year battle with long-term illness. Operations and hospital visits stole the joy from my life and made me question my own reason for existing. Some days I would have to fight *hard* just to pretend one day everything would be all right. Other days, the pain I felt was stronger than my own desire to live. I prayed, begging God to let me die. I would sit in church, looking at the cross in prayer, asking the Lord over and over what I'd done that I had to live like this. When would it all end? Hiding my pain, I would wipe my tears so neither Mama nor anyone else could see, but I continued to feel that, for me, there was no way out.

Even as a Christian, I felt death was the answer to all my problems. I would keep my Bible by my bed, and each night I'd read verses that told me what it would be like in heaven with God. I'd have a new body that would never be sick again. But suicide was *my* answer, not God's.

I know now that if I *had* committed suicide then, I would have missed the future God had planned for me. Through all those years of not understanding why I hurt, God was molding me with His loving hands, getting me ready for His purpose.

Loving God doesn't free us from pain or disappointment, but it allows us to have the assurance that He will go through all our trials with us. I know that God used my pain to do His work in me. I also learned to cast even my biggest heartaches on the Lord, and I found that His shoulders are stronger than mine. I discovered that He loves me more than I ever had imagined.

I have a special prayer, which came out of that time: "Lord, wrap your arms around me so that I can feel your loving presence in my life today." Those simple words, and the trust that goes with them, have carried me through so many tough days. But then, God is *always* there to carry us through when we call on His name.

In God's time, I began to understand. I moved from hopelessness to hope, from questions to understanding, from lost dreams to building new ones. And instead of taking my own life, I asked God to help me accept His reasons for why I should live.

Today, each time I hear the heart-breaking story of a young person who has tried to commit suicide or a sad account of a parent or friend of one who succeeded in killing himself, I feel a sense of responsibility to convince them suicide is not the answer.

But I quickly realize that there is nothing I can do or say on my own. God's love and strength are their hope. They need to believe that He can heal every broken heart and know that He is with us every day of our lives, giving us the courage to live.

If you have attempted suicide, if you have thought about killing yourself, or if you are close to someone who has, I ask you to give me the next few hours. Put your hand in mine and let me share with you the stories, the pain, and the promises of hope from other young people so much like yourself. Walk with me and believe, as I do, that when we are forced to face unbearable pain and disappointment, something bigger, brighter, and better can arise from the ashes of every hurt.

I have learned that the greatest secret to a rich, full, happy life is to seek and find God's plan for us with each sunrise. Each time the stars come out again, I want to be able to say, "I've done the best I could with what God gave me—His life for mine!"

Suicide is *not* the answer; God's *life* in you is.

Donalyn

Chapter 1

ARE YOU LISTENING, OR RUNNING?

O ne of the most important lessons I've ever learned came when I was lost and afraid. I wasn't lost in a strange city or the deep woods—I was lost *inside*. I didn't know where I was or how I got there. I prayed and prayed, but I couldn't see a way out to the happy, fun-filled life others seemed to be living. I was tired, and I didn't really want to quit—but I couldn't go on anymore.

When I finally stopped long enough to listen, the Lord began to teach me an important lesson. I'd been so busy thinking about *myself* and my own answers, that if the Lord *had* tried to answer my prayer, I couldn't have even heard Him.

There *are* solutions to every problem. Giving up isn't one of them. God's answers are not always the same as ours, though. He may have another path He wants us to follow.

But we will never know His reason for us to live if we don't *pray, wait,* and *listen.*

Chapter 2

SUICIDE IS FOREVER

Dear Donalyn,

There's one day I'll never be able to forget.

I just got home from school when the phone started ringing. It was a friend, telling me David had committed suicide.

I told her, "I don't believe you!" But I was already crying when I asked her to repeat what she said. I pressed my hands against my head, trying to stop the words that came back so loudly: "David is dead."

All I could do was scream, "No. I don't understand! I just don't understand! I just don't understand!"

I called Mom, but she couldn't leave work. I ran to my room and began to throw everything around. I couldn't stop crying. I thought I'd done something wrong.

When Mom got home, she just held me. I told her it was all my fault. David had asked me not to go away that weekend with her and the rest of the family. He wanted me to stay in town so we could go out together.

David had a lot of problems. He and his brother Tony were only nine months apart in age, and they used to do everything together. Less than a year ago, Tony was killed in a motorcycle accident. It seemed like David wouldn't let go of Tony's death. The last thing David said to me was, "'Till I call you Monday morning."

That night I cried myself to sleep. The next morning, I went to school because if I stayed home, I'd just go crazy. My friends gave me hugs and told me they were sorry.

I couldn't go to David's house. I saw his mom at the funeral home. She gave me a hug and told me the last few days of his life were happy because he'd spent them with me.

David had left his mom a letter, saying he hoped everyone would understand. He said he couldn't live without his brother. David's mom just kept saying they couldn't live without each other. She buried David next to Tony with a marker that said, "Forever Together."

After David's funeral, I kept going over the last week we were together. David had never given me any clues. He was depressed because, a few days earlier, it was Tony's birthday. I thought about our last date together and our last kiss. That night, David seemed to be feeling better. I thought about never having the chance to say goodbye again.

I found out through a close friend of ours that David was going to give me his class ring on Monday. All I could think about was that I never told him how much I cared for him. Why did this have to happen?

David used to talk about being in the Olympics. He was a great runner, and his room was full of trophies. At first, I talked about David twenty-four hours a day. Then some of my friends said something to me about it, and I began to feel like

I was getting on everyone's nerves. I don't talk about David anymore. I don't like to go places where we used to go together. There are too many memories.

When I think about David now, I don't think he really meant to do it. Sometimes I get depressed because I'd love to see him. I'll always want to know how long we would have lasted because we were so good together.

I'm dating someone else now, and I really like him. But I'm afraid to care about him because if something happens to him, I don't want to go through the same thing again.

There's a movie that I really love. This guy dies, but he comes back to see this girl that he loved just one last time. I'd give anything if that could be me.

Lisa

> "Why didn't he tell us?"
> "I don't know; I guess he couldn't."
> "If we could only have a second chance."
> "Suicide doesn't give second chances."

Dear Lisa,

I want you always to remember that you are *not* responsible for what someone else does with his life. Your searching heart was looking for the answer to David's death, but blaming yourself is not that answer.

You need to let go of your feelings of guilt and realize that David was responsible for his own actions. He'd been upset over his brother's death for a long time, and you had nothing to do with David committing suicide. At the time you left to go away with your parents, David may not even have been thinking about taking his own life. Since you weren't there, you don't even know the final events that took place before he died.

David knew how you felt about him, or he wouldn't have planned to give you his class ring. So you really did tell David that you cared about him—even if you didn't say it with words.

Lisa, we all need to communicate our feelings with someone who'll listen. When David first died, it was a shock for you and everyone else involved. All you could think about was David. It was only natural that you talked about him so much. When your friends brought it to your attention, they didn't mean that you could never bring up his name again. Because they care about you, they probably didn't want to see you hurt anymore. And maybe they thought that *not* talking about him would make it hurt less.

Don't assume that if you begin to care about someone else that you will lose him, too. The time you and David spent together was good, and good memories are wonderful. You need to find a place to rest those memories in your heart and go on with your life.

I think you're right about David not wanting to die. He wanted a way out from hurting so much, and he didn't know what else to do. David didn't realize that pain goes away, but suicide is forever.

I wish I could tell you there wouldn't be any more hurts or unanswered questions in your life. But I have had to bring many unanswered questions to God. And, through my tears, I wondered if I'd ever stop hurting. I *did* stop hurting, and I began to understand the work of God's hand in my life. Now I know that God was with me all along.

When I was growing up, my parents moved around a lot. I often attended more than one school in one year. I often wished

I had one home to grow up in and one town full of friends where I would never say goodbye.

As we grow up, we're building new dreams every day. Some of those dreams can come true, but some will never become a reality. When I lose a dream, I turn to the Lord and ask Him to put His desires in my heart. I know that the Lord has something good in store for me because He knows all about dreams. He also knows what's best for each one of us, so we need to trust Him.

The truth is, His dream for your life—even if you experience pain—will be the *best* dream of all.

One day at a time, I'm placing my life in God's hands.
I will lift my head high in His direction
as I bring Him my
disappointments,
broken dreams,
and
unanswered questions.
In His strength I can stand tall,
because God's timing is better than mine.
In God's time
I will better understand
all His plans for my life.
And I'll be thankful.
I take all my tomorrows and place them in God's hands.

Chapter 3

A God of Second Chances

Mrs. Pate asked me to follow her down the hall. There was a confident assurance in the sound of her footsteps. When we walked into her office, I sat in the chair across from her desk. It wasn't until that moment that we really had a chance to look each other in the face.

She was an attractive woman, perhaps in her early forties. Her brown, short hair softly framed her face. She had eyes that were warm and friendly, making me feel comfortable in her presence. They showed no sign of the hardship I had heard she'd just gone through.

At the same time I was checking her out, I could sense she was not only looking *at* me, but *inside* me.

And then, the heartache appeared on her face as a deep sigh opened up the door of her heart. She allowed me to enter, breaking the silence between us as she placed the past few years of her son's life in my hands. "There are many sides to hurting. You would never have thought something like this could happen in a town with only a post office, a grocery store, and a garage. But it did."

She went on to explain that it all seemed to begin with Brad's car accident. He was sixteen and going through a "show-off" stage. Once, driving too fast, he had a terrible accident that left him with three hundred stitches in his head. "While Brad was still in the hospital, he began saying he couldn't remember anything. The doctor assured us that nothing was wrong with him. But he kept telling us he had a hard time remembering.

"When he went back to school, his old friends made fun of him. It wasn't long before I noticed he was making new friends. But I thought, in time, things would be back to normal. I didn't know that those friends accepted him on one term only—anyone who got high with them was 'okay.'

"Soon he was forging checks and stealing things out of the house to get the money he needed to support his drug habit. Lying became a daily routine. His grades dropped. When he quit school, his father and I weren't surprised.

"As Brad drifted further and further from us, he seemed lost and haunted. Looking for a way to help him, we sent him to a drug rehab center. But their idea of 'help' was just to give him legal drugs.

"When he came back home, we weren't prepared for his newest means to get the drugs he wanted. Although he was only sixteen, the state police began to slip him money, which he used for drugs. They used him as an undercover narcotics agent. We knew something strange was going on. So one night we followed him and forced him to tell us the truth. We stood at a pay phone as he called his partner at the police station.

We were outraged that the state police used a young boy as a means to make their drug busts. The police warned us that if we went public with what they were doing, the drug pushers would have Brad killed.

"But when the police could no longer support his addiction, our son turned back to robbing. When he was caught stealing cars, I warned him that if he stole another car, he couldn't come back home. In the time he took to laugh at my warning, he stole another car.

"I should have known I wasn't talking to my son," she said, her eyes filling with tears, "but only to the shell of a human being. His 'food' consisted of drugs of only the highest quality—coke, heroin, acid. His only thought was, *How can I get my next fix?*

"What happened to the son I once knew?" Mrs. Pate pleaded. "The one who had a bright awareness in his eyes. The one who loved life. The son I miss and would give anything to hold again. Brad didn't just *live* life, he *experienced* it. Sure, he had a strong will, but he also had compassion for others. He had a way about him that always melted my heart.

"Knowing these qualities were still alive somewhere inside Brad—and that we loved him—my husband and I sold our home to raise the money we needed to help him get rid of his craving for drugs. Still, we began to feel as though we'd failed him in some way—but we didn't know how. We felt guilty, and so helpless.

"Brad tried to kill himself. Not once, but several times. When a serious attempt to overdose failed, he told us, 'If I can't kill myself, I can *have* it done by someone else.' So he set up an armed robbery. When the police surrounded him, he walked out without taking anything, hoping they would shoot him. But they didn't—they took him to jail.

"Something inside of me still said, *Don't give up on him.* When I went to jail to see him, he was going through withdrawal. I cried and put my hands against the glass wall that separated us. He told me he loved me more than I'll ever know—but I should give up and let him die. When I left the jail that afternoon, I knew there was only one answer: God.

"This nightmare had been going on for two and a half years. If God had kept my son alive this long, I knew He had something special planned for his life. I believed God would answer my prayer to save Brad's life.

"Then a minister started coming to the jail. He continued to tell Brad, day after day, about God's love. He said God had the healing power to help him put away his drug addiction for the rest of his life. One night, Brad called me. He was reading a Bible. He said he'd accepted Christ and that he was ready to accept his legal punishment. At nineteen, he was facing sixty years in jail.

"But you know, a strange thing happened. While he prepared for his trial, a doctor's examination revealed that the car accident did affect Brad's thinking and reasoning ability. Brad felt as if a huge burden had been lifted from his shoulders. *Finally,* someone believed him. The more I went to jail to see him, the more I believed he was sincere in accepting Christ. He wasn't trying to live by his own wits anymore. He was depending on God's help.

"Before Brad's trial, we read from God's Word: 'You are prisoners of sin, every one of you. And prisoners don't have rights, but Jesus has every right there is! So if Jesus sets you free you will indeed be free' (John 8:34–36).

"When God gave Brad a new birth, I knew that whatever we had to face, we would make it. Brad was sentenced to just one year! Today, he's out of jail, and he's trying hard to be the young man God wants him to be. He's thankful to be alive and thankful that God gave Him another chance at life.

"To be honest," Mrs. Pate confided, "I almost threw away my relationship with God because of the pain we were going through. But instead I turned my life *toward* God. And He's used our pain to reach out to others who have gone through the same heartaches."

When I looked at my watch, *four hours* had quickly passed. She'd taken me into the most private areas of her life. My heart had ached as I'd watched her cry.

And now, with a special glow in her eyes, she said, "Today I can understand how God's hand was working in our lives. And I can only thank Him for being a God of second chances."

She finished, and I got up to hug her as we said goodbye. And I silently thanked God for the amazing way He works, even in the most difficult times of our lives.

> Looking for a way out,
> I took a chance on getting high.
> But it didn't change a thing.
> There are no perfect people and no perfect places,
> even when you are stoned.
> Getting high all the time
> ended up being a lot of trash.
> And the places it takes you—
> you don't want to go.

Chapter 4

SOMETHING WORTH LIVING FOR

I never thought I'd make it through those rollercoaster years. One day I'd feel like everything was all right, and the next day I'd feel like my whole world was caving in. I had a hard time dealing with my own anger. I'd be angry at the world because I didn't think life was fair. And I would be angry at myself if I felt like I wasn't good enough. I found myself trapped in a whirlwind of confusing notions, spiraling downward.

One day my anger turned on me. I tried to take my own life. At the time, I thought, "If I die, then all my problems will be solved." But I really didn't think about being *dead*.

I wish someone had brought me here, to this cemetery. I think it would have made me feel like there had to be a better way than giving up and dying. I can't say graveyards make me feel good. I've never seen anyone singing as they left a funeral.

One day someone cared enough to tell me about Jesus and how He loved me so much that He died on the cross so I could have life. I started praying about everything. I even asked Him to help show me how to control my anger. I don't have all the answers, but prayer changed my life.

I still have a lot of growing up to do, but I know I can make it with Jesus in my life. I want to leave this world with people saying something more about me than, "He's the guy who killed himself."

Chapter 5

DECISIONS FROM THE HEART

"May I have your attention, please?" Miss Moore announced.

She was a stout woman, a little taller than her students, with rosy cheeks and a head full of silver hair. She reminded the girls of Mrs. Claus at Christmas. During the past twenty years, she had taught personal health classes for the pregnant teens at the home. She was old enough to retire, but no one could imagine the home without her—even though the girls made fun of her old-fashioned ways. The girls were like grandchildren to her, and she sincerely cared for all of them. They, in turn, returned her love above all the other teachers.

"I have a surprise for you," Miss Moore announced with anticipation. "We have a special guest today. What she has to share will be important to all of us. Her name is Candice Shepard."

An attractive woman in her middle twenties walked to the front of the class wearing a blue dress with matching heels. Her long blonde hair fell across her shoulders.

Miss Moore got up from her desk and took a seat at the back of the room. The woman stood quietly, waiting for full attention from all the girls in the class. Then, with a warm smile, she began.

"I've been asked to come and talk to you about adoption. All of you have made the right choice to carry your child full term. I applaud your decision. I have something to share with you. The beginning of my story isn't very good. I let fear and guilt lead me into making a terrible mistake, and because of the choices I made, it has affected me every day of my life." With everyone's attention, she began her story.

"I grew up listening to my parents constantly fighting. When I was thirteen, they separated, and my mother began working full-time. After my two older sisters left for college, I often found myself preparing my own meals and attending to the household chores while my mother was working late.

"Each night, I'd start my homework with good intention to get it all done, but it never seemed to work out that way. I couldn't keep focused, and no matter how hard I tried to stay focused, I'd spend my time talking to friends online or texting on my phone. My mother didn't get home from work until late, and she often found me asleep on my bed with my books by my side and my homework unfinished.

"I was lonely and hated coming home to an empty house, and I missed my sisters. The more I was left alone, the more I became bored and restless. I invited friends over after school, but Mom wasn't a real fan of that idea.

"I couldn't date; my mother said I wasn't ready. When I asked, she only told me she would let me know when it was time.

"One afternoon, while looking for something to do, I walked into my sisters' room and began to try on some of their clothes. There was a difference in our ages, but all three of us were the same size. I was often mistaken for being closer to their age than my own.

"I couldn't help but notice, in my sisters' clothes, I looked more like eighteen than my real age of fifteen.

"On this day, I couldn't stand being left in the house all alone, so I called Julie, a friend of mine, because she was home alone too.

"'Hey, you want to go with me to Kelly's?'

"'Sure, I'll go. I'll meet you in front of your house in five minutes,' Julie replied.

"There were picnic tables outside at Kelly's, and after the dinner crowd left, the restaurant served fruit smoothies and milkshakes until it closed around ten o'clock.

"When we walked into Kelly's, we were giggling loudly enough for everyone to notice our entrance. I caught the eye of a friend of my sisters, sitting alone at the end of the counter. He was a freshman in college and wasn't usually hanging around town during the week.

"We glanced his way and walked past him, smiling, and then we pulled out a couple of stools as close as we could get for not being invited to join him. I was a little uncomfortable as I could feel him staring at me. His name was Ronnie, and I remembered him from high school. He was cute then and seemed even cuter now.

"There was no mistaking his muscular frame, baby-blue eyes, and little-boy smile. I could hardly believe he was even looking my way. He wasn't just looking at me; he was staring. My heart skipped a beat as I watched him get up from his chair and place himself right between me and my friend.

"With irresistible charm, he leaned over and whispered in my ear, 'When did you grow up?'

'"When you began to notice,' I giggled.

"Ronnie leaned in a little more and braced his hands on the counter.

"'I thought you left for college. What are you doing here?' I asked.

"'I did, but my family needed me closer to home, so I transferred to the junior college for one semester.' I could tell his voice was full of mixed emotions and something more was going on.

"'I'm sorry,' I said, wishing I had never asked.

"'Why are you two here?'

"'We just wanted to get out of the house. I was bored, and Julie came with me.'

"'I was bored, too,' Julie said as she noticed the attraction between the two of us, which she wasn't a part of.

"'I have a couple of hours with nothing else to do. Would you girls like to go for a ride with me?' Ronnie asked.

"I cut a look at Julie, showing her how excited I was by the invitation.

"'I've got stuff I can do. You go on,' Julie said.

"'No, I won't go without you,' I said and then leaned behind Ronnie and mouthed, 'Please come with me.'

"'All right, I'll go, but you owe me one,' Julie answered loudly.

"'I have to be back by seven,' I said.

"'I *better* be back by seven,' replied Julie.

"With his promise to return on time, we followed him outside. Ronnie drove out of town and stopped at an open field at a local national park. We all agreed a walk would be fun. I paid close attention as he helped me and Julie out of the car. *He's so nice*, I thought.

"Ronnie led us on a path through the park, and we climbed to the top of a large rock, standing in silence and looking across the valley below.

"'It's really beautiful up here.' I spoke the words we were all thinking.

"Ronnie searched around to find a resting place below the rock. Julie stretched out as if she was trying to catch some sun and acted like she wasn't interested. I listened patiently while Ronnie talked about school and his reasons for coming home. His father was seriously ill, but he assured me he planned to return to college when his father's health improved. I wasn't sure if he was trying to convince himself or if he was trying to tell me he wasn't going to be around very long.

"The afternoon went by quickly. On the ride home, Ronnie made the choice to drop Julie off first. When he got to my house, he asked if he could see me again. His invitation caught me completely off guard. I panicked.

"I can't believe this! I thought. *I'll never see him again if I tell him my mom won't let me date. What am I going to say?* Determined to make this happen, I was certain I could pull this off without my mom's permission. *She's working; she'll never know,* I told myself.

"'I get home from school around quarter of four. Call me if that's a good time for you.'

"Ronnie did call the next day, and we sat on her front porch and talked for hours. I hung onto his every word. Ronnie came several times during the week, and it wasn't long before I invited him in to watch a movie or play a video game. Some afternoons we went for a walk and talked about everything. I was certain I had never met anyone more wonderful than Ronnie Clark.

When my mother asked what I did each afternoon, I would twist the truth a little and not mentioned Ronnie's name.

"Everything had changed since I met him. I looked forward to his visits, and he told me he felt the same way. I was certain if my mother knew, Ronnie wouldn't be allowed to come over, and I couldn't bear the thought of not seeing him again. I didn't feel like I wasn't being dishonest. I just didn't mention his name or bring up his visits.

"In our afternoons together, he was my first kiss, the first boy I had held hands with, and the first one to hear the secrets I had never shared before. I was there for him to listen patiently while he talked about his father's illness and how he planned to return to school.

"Ronnie had a part time job, working weekends, so it caught me off guard when he asked to take me out on a Saturday night. I didn't want to lie, not to him, so I confessed and told him my mother didn't allow me to date, not until I was sixteen. He was surprised but told me that I was more understanding and mature than most of the girls my age. After all, I had been his sounding board for the last several weeks and had made things a little easier as he dealt with his father's declining health and the pressures of school and trying to help his mom.

"'You have been more support to me than anyone at school. You're a lot older than you think. I don't know if my dad is going to be like this forever or if one day I'll come home and he will be dead. Life just happens, and you can't always be prepared. You might think you are, but everything can change in a day.'

"'Are you scared?' I asked.

"'Yes, but then I have to believe my father is going to get well and life is going to be the way it used to be. Cancer affects everyone in the family; it's like this fog that covers your eyes, and you can't see. The truth is, you really don't want to see or know if the patient's life is going to end soon. You can't see in front of you, so you don't know what's ahead. I see my dad living in pain, and I feel helpless. I don't know what I would do if I didn't have you.' Ronnie had a way of making me feel like I was the most important person in his life.

"I understood the heartache of his father's illness; he understood my parents' divorce. The more insecure we both felt, the closer we became. Ronnie didn't give up wanting to see me on the weekends, but he agreed to see me only after school with the hope my mother would eventually change her mind.

"One evening, after my mother came home from work, I told her about Ronnie. What was the worst thing that could happen? If she said I couldn't see him anymore, things would go on the same, and I would meet him after school. But maybe, just maybe, she would understand and trust me enough to let me go out on a date, a real date.

"'Mom, I really like Ronnie, and I didn't know how to tell you. It just happened. If you met him, you would like him too. I'll be sixteen in a month. He's only two years older than me, but we get along so well. He asked me out, and I really want to go. It's so close to my birthday. Couldn't I go?'

"My mother knew if she didn't allow me to see him, I would still find a way to be with him, and she didn't want us to see each other in secret. Mom gave Ronnie permission to come over once a week when she was home after school and on the weekends.

"Ronnie took advantage of the approved visits, but we also continued to see each other more often. Spending time alone in the house gave no boundaries to the physical attraction between us. It wasn't long before Ronnie led me through each step of physical intimacy; I followed his lead. While he was kissing me, he began to touch me in ways I had never been touched before, and I trusted him.

"Although no words were spoken between us, I knew he was going to continue until there was nothing to hold us back. One afternoon, Ronnie held me very close and began to remove my clothes as he whispered, 'I love you.'

"I hesitated for a moment, but I tried not to think about what was happening; I only wanted to be caught in the passion I felt for him. 'I love you, too,' I whispered.

"When the sex was over, Ronnie was surprised to find out I was a virgin. He apologized—as if sex was just an argument that happened between us. It wasn't what he said, but how he said it that made me feel used.

"'I love you, Ronnie. I want us to be together forever.'

"'I love you too, but I'm not ready for a serious relationship. I have college, and I'm not sure what's going on with my dad. This isn't what I want right now.'

"I watched him look around the room, making sure he wasn't leaving anything behind.

"'Your mom will be home soon. I better go.'

"I didn't know the boy standing before me, the way he looked at me, the tone in his voice. His urgency to leave was so unlike him.

"Pretending not to let his actions bother me, I wrapped my arms around him; my eyes begged for him to return the affection. He knew what I wanted, so he leaned toward me and gently kissed me goodbye. I watched him leave, taking my heart with him. No one had to tell me; I knew. Things would be different between us.

"Two days went by without a word. On the third day, I called him. Ronnie told me his father was worse and he was busy helping his mom. I understood, but he could have said he missed me, or he could have called, but he didn't say anything I wanted to hear.

"I hoped he cared enough not to want to hurt me, but he had to know my heart was broken. I heard him say he loved me, but that was then. Now I believed he said it for sex; it wasn't for me. *How could I have been so stupid?* I asked myself.

"Days passed into weeks without a word from Ronnie. I told myself it didn't matter, but it did. I made excuses for him, but nothing made me feel better. *He disappeared from my life as quickly as he came in,* I thought.

"My mother tried to help me realize we were both young, and at my age, there would be other boys—until I met the right one. But I knew my mother didn't know I had given myself to him, and it was more than a crush. I was physically and emotionally involved beyond what I was ready to handle. Then there was the guilt of what had happened.

"I will never forget the day I realized my period was late. I kept telling myself it was only a few days, and then the days turned into weeks. No one needed to tell me. I knew I was pregnant." Candice held the girls' attention as she shared her story.

"Not knowing what to do, I called Ronnie. I heard his father had died, and I thought, *Maybe he will be glad to hear from me.* His mother innocently explained Ronnie had returned to school.

"When I asked when he would be home, she assured me he wouldn't be home again until next summer. The phone call confirmed I was on my own. Alone and frightened, I went to see a doctor, only to have my fears confirmed. I was pregnant. I paid little attention as the doctor began to explain how I needed to care for myself and the baby.

"Mother was right. I wasn't ready to date, and I knew I was not ready to have this baby.

"Returning home, I tearfully opened the phone book, seeking any information on pregnancy counseling. I chose a clinic not far from home. My fingers trembled as I dialed the numbers on my cell phone. The woman's voice was understanding as she urged me to come into the clinic so we could talk. Desperate for help, I left right away. When I arrived, I silently sat in a waiting room filled with faces of other young girls, ranging in age from thirteen to twenty-two. *They must be pregnant too*, I thought.

"It seemed like hours before I heard the receptionist call my name. Fear had taken over my heart as I followed the woman down a long, gray hall. She opened a door to enter a small room. Hanging on the wall were posters giving all the reasons a woman had control over body.

"The poster used the word *fetus* and referred to it with no more emotion than a cyst in your stomach. Not wanting to read anymore, I placed my head in my hands. Desperately, I waited for someone to walk through the door. When the door swung open, a woman in her middle forties pushed herself through the room and wasted no time. Direct in her conversation, she introduced herself to me and led me through two pages of questions. I cried as I slowly gave her my name, age, length of pregnancy, parents' names, and their knowledge of my pregnancy. Several times during our conversation, she assured me it would be all over before I knew it.

"'You can go on with your life as if nothing happened,' the woman assured me.

"I wanted to believe her, but I felt lost in a maze, clawing to find my way out. There was no one I could call for help. The woman went on to explain the procedure. The words meant nothing to me. When asked if I had any questions, I shook my head no, quickly picked up the pen, and signed the papers in front of me.

"When everything was signed, the woman handed me an appointment card with the date and time I would return. I walked out of the room, glancing over the papers the woman placed in my hands.

"I had lied about my age, and no one questioned me. I wouldn't have to wait long; I was to return the next morning. The nurse explained they treat the young girls before the older ones because it's too much stress on them to wait. Everything was planned, yet I felt sick inside, not relieved. I knew what was going to happen, but I couldn't bring myself to say the word. Even so, I felt the word *abortion* in every cell of my body.

"The next day, I told my mother I wasn't feeling well and wanted to stay home from school. She agreed and promised to call later. Mixed emotions filled my head. I wished my parents were still together and things weren't so hard on my mother. Mom had to work long shifts just to help pay the bills. As I finished getting ready and raised my arm to brush my hair, I sank to the floor and cried. *It's all my fault, and I have to make things right! We can't afford a baby.*

"Outside, the rain fell hard against my umbrella. Holding tightly to the handle, I started walking to the clinic. I kept my head down, and for some silly reason, I stomped my foot in the water puddles as I walked. My pants were soaked, and I laughed at my silliness. For one moment, I forgot where I was going and why. Then, I arrived at my destination and stared at the front door.

"*I've got to go in. It's all going to be over soon, like it never happened*, I thought. Taking a deep breath, I repeated the words out loud, 'As if it never happened.'

"Once inside, I walked up to the receptionist and whispered my name. The woman behind the front desk acknowledged my presence and soon a nurse asked me to follow her to a preparation room down the hall.

"I waited for about five minutes before the same nurse I had spoken with the day before entered the room. She asked me to remove my clothes and put on a hospital gown.

"'It won't be much longer now,' she said as she patted me lovingly on my knee before leaving the room.

"My hands shook as I slowly unbuttoned my blouse. I felt numb inside, going through the motions. I put on the gown and sat on the edge of the chair, waiting for someone to return to the room. Every second seemed like an eternity. It was all surreal to me, and I wanted to keep it that way. I jumped when the door opened to a woman I had never met before.

"'Hello, my name is Kate. I'm going to give you a shot. It's going to make you sleepy. Don't worry; you're going to be fine and on your way home in just a little while.'

"I felt the sharp burn of the needle entering my hip. *Please let me go to sleep right away*, I thought. I was ready for anything that would take away the fear of what I was doing. As the nurse left the room, I turned over and pressed my back against the table and began to shiver. Tears filled my eyes as I stared at an empty ceiling. It was only moments later when I began to release my fear and relax as I gave into the medication and closed my eyes. I heard someone come into the room, but I didn't respond.

"'Candice, this is Kate again. I am going to get you ready for Dr. Caron. You need to help me pull yourself down and get your feet in the stirrups on the table.'

"I was awake just enough to pull my body down and place my legs into the straps. I wanted to return to sleep. I could feel the nurse strap me onto the table. Even if I wanted to move, I couldn't, and I honestly didn't care. I felt a cloth being draped over my waist and legs.

"'Candice, I am Dr. Caron. We are getting ready to get started. You are going to be just fine,' she said, placing her hand on Candice's shoulder.

"After introducing herself, the doctor instructed her assistant to place the surgical instruments on the small tray beside her. I could hear the doctor talking, but it was like a dream.

"'Forceps, saline,' the doctor said.

"I jerked a little as Dr. Caron lifted the sheet below my knees. 'Oh!' I shouted.

"The numbing medication the doctor had administered helped with the pain, but I could still feel the sensation of suction inside my body. I froze when I felt a ripping sensation inside of me.

"'You're going to feel a strong pulling sensation,' Dr. Caron announced.

"What she didn't tell me was the suction machine she used worked like a vacuum cleaner, tearing the baby and placenta to pieces.

"The inside of my stomach felt strange, and the pain I felt seemed to go beyond my stomach into my whole body. I felt hot, and sweat covered my body, and then, what seemed like forever was finally over.

"'It's all over. You did just fine,' the doctor reassured me.

"I watched as the nurse left the room with a small, covered tray. Another nurse entered and released the straps from below my chest and legs.

"'Is it really over? I'm not pregnant anymore?' I asked.

"'You're not pregnant anymore,' the nurse confirmed."

Making sure she had the full attention of all the girls, Candice said, "Instead of relief, I felt a deep sadness I wasn't prepared for. I got up from the table and dressed. I was told it was over, but it wasn't over. It was true that I wasn't pregnant anymore, but what they didn't tell me was that every day I would regret the choice I had made. The loss of a child I did not carry and the life I took would always leave a sadness in my heart of what could have been."

The classroom was quiet as the young girls listened to Candice share her abortion with them. "I had taken a life to hide my shame because I was afraid."

Candice looked across the room with tear-filled eyes. "From the moment of conception, life begins. At twelve weeks, the baby is fully developed, with toes and fingers, ears, and eyelids. I've never forgotten the baby I aborted. This is what I've learned: we can't replace our past; it's always with us."

Candice removed her jacket and raised the sleeves of her shirt to show the girls her wrists. "I know this because I have tried to kill myself by cutting my wrists at least six times. You can look closely at my arms and count the scars. No, I didn't die, but I wanted to take my own life.

"An abortion doesn't eliminate the fact you were once pregnant. Fear should never be a reason to end another's life. I was afraid and never asked for help. I never gave my mom or anyone else the opportunity to help me look at other options. No one told me there were millions of couples waiting to adopt a baby. No one warned me that you could suffer from depression after an abortion. No one told me I would always feel the pain of my abortion.

"Every time I see a sweet baby smile, I'm reminded of the child I aborted. Every time I see a family together with small children, I'm reminded of the life I could have chosen for my child. The one lesson the abortion has taught me is how sacred life is. God gives us free will to make our own choices, but on our own, we can make a mess of things. There is no escaping the consequences of our choices.

"I want you to know what happened after I came home from the clinic. I couldn't hide my pain or heavy bleeding from my mother. She rushed me to the hospital, only to have a doctor explain what I couldn't tell her. I had to have surgery to repair the internal damage from the abortion.

"When the truth came out, my mother was deeply hurt, but she never stopped loving me. I know now she would have helped me make the right choice, but I never gave her the opportunity. She blamed herself, but I had no one to blame but myself. I felt so much guilt. And that's when I began to cut myself." The girls in the room glanced again at the scars on her wrists.

"With counseling and the love of my mom, I found out that God's grace is for all of us, not just some of us, and He loves me enough to forgive me and help me be the woman he always wanted me to be.

"I wasn't ready to be a mother as a pregnant teen. It's hard to be a parent when you still need so much parenting yourself.

There will be times in your life when you feel alone and afraid, and I hope you will remember God is always there for you.

"I'm proud to tell you, I graduated from high school and went to college. I met a wonderful man and got married. After college, I fell in love with the right guy, and I waited until we were married to have sex. I finally got things right, but the consequences of my choices had a lasting effect. My doctor told me I would never carry another child. My heart ached because I couldn't become pregnant, but from my pain came an answer to my prayers and my greatest blessing.

"I will always be grateful to the pregnant teen who gave birth to my son. I admire her courage to give her child a home when she wasn't ready to be a parent. My son was brought into my family through adoption, but he is no longer adopted. He is just as much a part of me as if I gave birth to him myself. There is no difference in my love, and I am the mother to the most amazing little boy.

"It's taken years of praying and walking with God to stand before you. I made a mistake, but God has forgiven me and taken my shame. He never stopped loving me because His love for us is unconditional. Today I help young women understand there is another choice. I understand where they are because I was a pregnant teen.

"I don't think there's anyone in this class who doesn't want to be somewhere else. If you are honest and were given another choice, I know you would have waited. You are here at the home because you chose to carry your child to raise or to give birth for another family. Both are decisions of the heart God will honor.

"Recently, a young girl shared with me; she was thinking about getting an abortion. After talking with her, she chose adoption. When we talked about her family, the memories of her own young childhood came rushing back. She recalled fun and happy memories with a loving mother and father. That night, she went home and shared her pregnancy with her parents and told them her choice. She wanted the baby she carried to have what she had, a home with a mother and a father, full of happy memories.

"I've been told several of you are considering adoption. Maybe you don't have happy memories, or one parent raised you. Maybe you had a parent who abandoned you, and you feel like you will be abandoning this child if you choose adoption. You couldn't be more wrong. Adoption isn't walking away from your child; it's providing for your child in another way. You choose life for a child, a chance to be someone special in this world and to live with purpose. God has a plan for all of us, and His plans go on for the rest of our lives.

"Look at me. I was a restless young girl who wanted to be so much older than I was. I was wishing my life away. I wanted to date and be free to go and come as I pleased. I was certain I knew more than my mom when it came to boys and dating. I didn't need anyone to tell me what to do. I had all the right answers for myself."

One of the girls from the back of the room raised her hand. "If you had to do it all again, what would you do?"

"I would have waited. If you were asking me about the abortion, I would have chosen adoption. Children are not ours to own. I wasn't ready to be a mother. I still needed my mother. If I kept the baby, it would have only been because I wanted Ronnie to come back in my life. But who knows what he would have done? I would be making a choice out of my own selfishness. You make these kinds of mistakes when you're young. The time we were together, both of us were very vulnerable. We were going through a lot, and we turned to each other. He was losing his father to death, and I lost mine through my parents' divorce."

"Tell us more about your son," a voice from the back of the room interjected.

"There isn't a day I take him for granted. Each day I look into his eyes, I see the visible evidence of God's love and the miracle He brought into my life—a miracle I prayed for. He's a happy little boy who keeps me going. In him I see the evidence of answered prayer and how much God loves me because he is the child I prayed for.

"You don't have to give birth to a child to be a mother. So many young teens have good intentions, and they keep their babies, but their grandparents raise the child. Some children end up in foster care because the mother realizes, after the fact, that she is not ready for the responsibility of raising a child. However, she lets guilt prevent her from giving the child up for adoption. Whatever you do, don't let pride or guilt make your choice. Don't let your past make you feel like you don't have a full life ahead of you. God can use your mistakes and turn your life around for His good.

"Think about this: God chose Mary and Joseph to be the adoptive parents of Jesus. How could it be any better than to be in the same company as Jesus Christ himself?

"Go from this place in your life and make choices that are right for you and the child you carry. I see a room full of beautiful girls, full of possibilities. I know, without any doubt, God has a plan for each one of you. Whatever your choice will be, let it be for the right reasons, and let your life be full of hope for a future with God in it. God's love for us fills every void we might have so we don't have to run after what the world has to offer us. Jesus died on a cross to give us forgiveness for our sins, and His heart is full of grace for us. Whatever you go through, God will help you.

"Remember Isaiah 41:13: For I am the Lord your God who takes hold of your right hand and says to you, 'Do not fear; I will help you.'"

Note: According to the Guttmacher Institute, among fifteen- to nineteen-year-old pregnant teens, 29 percent of pregnancies end in abortion.

Chapter 6

Reaching for God

Donalyn,

I am fifteen years old, and I have been cutting myself for over a year. I have never told anyone until this letter. I wear long sleeves and pants to hide my cuts and scars. I was sexually abused when I was twelve by my best friend's father. It went on for a year. I confided in my big sister about what he was doing to me, and she told my parents. I thought they would protect me, but instead, my parents told me to keep my mouth shut about it. They said nobody would believe it. The previous year, his niece had filled charges against him, and he got out of them. My parents were afraid the bad publicity could hurt my father's business. It was never talked about again after that day, and everybody pretended nothing had ever happened to me.

A year later, both my older brother and sister moved out and went to live with two different relatives in two different states. My mom also moved away, leaving my little sister and me with our dad. Mom has never tried to call or see us. I stay to myself, and I cry all the time. I can't stand to look at myself in the mirror. It makes me feel sick to my stomach. I feel unloved and unwanted. I often think everything that has happened to me is somehow my fault and I am being punished.

Growing up, I used to go to church three days a week with one of my neighbors, but I stopped going when the abuse started. I am mad at God! Why wouldn't He protect me? Why did he let those things happen to me? In my eyes, God turned his back on me, just like my mom and dad did.

The first time I hurt myself, I cut my wrist, wanting to die. I had tried to kill myself multiple times with pills. This time I planned on slitting my wrists. After I made several deep cuts, the burning and stinging was the only thing I could feel. It took my mind off of all the pain I felt inside. I have been cutting myself ever since. I have tried to stop, but it doesn't last long. Even though I know the physical pain is only temporary, it is the only way I know how to stop all the painful memories that continue to play over and over in my mind. At least I can breathe for a short time. Isn't that better than never breathing at all? I don't know what to do anymore. I feel lost and broken.

Anna

Anna,

You've kept a very serious event in your life a secret. You also began to believe the lie that your own hurt didn't matter. Sexual abuse as a young girl is painful and you can carry that pain for the rest of your life—unless you decide not to believe the lies of your past.

Now that you are older, what you do about this is your choice.

You have the choice of letting this hold you back or accepting the truth that this was not your fault. You can decide that you are not going to let your abuse continue to pull you down. It's important to know there is no shame in asking for help to deal with your feelings. Asking for help means you care enough about yourself and your future to get better.

You lost your mother and were separated from a brother and sister, just when you needed your family most. I'm certain you felt alone. To help you deal with this pain, you first need a plan. We all can change things about ourselves, and the more you practice this plan, the better you will become at it. The more you understand the feelings that make you want to harm yourself, the closer you will get to finding other ways to solve your problems and deal with hurt in your life. The next time you feel like cutting yourself because you are feeling a great deal of pain or have simply had a bad day, you can use your plan to help you cope. When you hurt and you want to cut yourself, do one of the following instead:

1. Go for a walk and take your music to sing along while you're walking.
2. Tell yourself you are a strong young woman and you have the power to stop this. Remind yourself of all the good things that are true of you. Dream about a vision of something you want to do or become when you grow up. Ask God to help you see your gifts and your talents. The Bible tells us that when we seek God, he will answer us (Deut. 4:29). Christ will help you see the beautiful young woman He sees when he looks at you.

3. Do you love to read? Stop what you are doing and go somewhere quiet and read. Whatever activity you enjoy doing, take the time to do this for yourself.

4. Call or visit someone you love. I used to go over to my grandmother's house, and by the time I left her home, I had a whole new world in front of me.

5. Clean your room. Oh, yes, I am suggesting cleaning your room. When you clean your room, you can see the result of your work.

Come up with your own list, and let it be your plan whenever you feel like cutting yourself. In time, you will have the power to overcome the feelings of wanting to harm yourself.

You are so much more than someone who cuts herself. You are a beautiful young woman, and God has a plan for your life that only you can fulfill. Don't let the lies of your past or the fears of today stop you from showing up for God's blessing for your life.

You can do this. I know you can, and I'm praying for you. Your life is worth living, and I know God's best for you is just around the corner.

Dear Donalyn,

I felt like I was a complete failure. I couldn't sleep or eat or study for days. Everything was wrong, and there was a haze over my mind so that I couldn't come up with a plan to make things right.

I was ashamed of so many things. I had done something I knew was wrong, and I felt really guilty. But there was no one who would understand, no one to talk with about it. There was no one to say the words I wanted to hear: "You're forgiven. Your whole future doesn't have to be ruined." I felt completely out of control. I tried hard to cover up my feelings of guilt and depression, but that didn't help. Sometimes I would end up crying in the stairwell between classes. Then I would try to touch up my makeup and get to my next class, only to sit in the back of class with a fake smile.

Finally, my mind rebelled along with my heart. I'd always been a top student, but I could only look helplessly at my books. I couldn't concentrate enough to study. All I could think of were my problems; this new preoccupation caused my grades to crash. Friends tried to help, knowing these grades were very important to my college plans. They sat for hours, trying to study with me, but it seemed nothing was sinking in.

Then came the test that could make the difference between a really good college and a so-so school. Trying to answer questions was hopeless—my mind had gone blank. I finally surrendered my answer booklet, then went outside to wait for the results.

I saw all my future plans crumble when they told me, "You didn't pass."

I had to get far away. I felt like I'd failed at everything that was important to me, and I couldn't stand the pain of it all any longer. I drove for hours and finally ended up in a crowded parking lot. I was sure that no one would notice my little car until it was too late. I laid down on the back seat with a soda and a bag of pills. I'd carefully researched which combination of pills to take, so I would *not* be a failure at suicide, too. But instead of taking them, I just laid there for hours, crying. Finally, I fell asleep from exhaustion.

When I woke up, I began sipping the soda. I looked out at the stars. For the first time, the universe seemed to unfold in perfect order and sequence for me. I began to remember lessons I'd learned in Sunday school when I was little. God created the universe. He created me, and maybe He did have a plan for my life.

At first, I was reluctant to believe. Then, just a little, I realized that God was my Father and He truly cares for me. I felt a growing sense of wonder at the vast power of God's control over stars and space and time. I felt humbled at the thought that God—the Creator of these stars and planets—looked down on one small planet, at one small person—me—and cared.

I threw away the bag of pills.

Kathy

There's Nothing Broken He Can't Repair

"Those broken baskets look like my life."

"When I first looked, I didn't see the broken parts because the grass was hiding them."

"Those baskets can still be used if someone would repair them. It makes me think about how Jesus repairs and replaces our broken pieces so we can go on to be everything He wants us to be."

Dear Kathy,

I'm so glad you discovered on your own that you didn't need the bag of pills.

After all, who said you were a complete failure? Just you. The words we allow into our minds can do one of two things: drown us in our own self-pity or encourage us to make it through the tough times. Sometimes we aren't even aware of the language that surrounds our lives. Have you listened to a song and liked the beat of the music, but when you stopped to really listen to the words, they brought you down?

I'm not surprised you failed your exam. You said yourself you couldn't focus enough to study. But *you tried.* That's what's important. Failing an exam isn't the end of the world. At least you know why you failed. It's a lot easier to make a change when you know why something happened. When we make mistakes and know why they happened, we can work harder to keep them from happening again. The grade isn't as important as being able to say, "I really did my best."

Often when we feel ashamed of something we've done, we build a wall that keeps everyone out—even the Lord. Something inside says, *I can't talk about what's wrong.* So what do we do? We hide and refuse to let anyone get close to us. We don't want anyone to touch us when we hurt.

One afternoon, my younger brother fell off his bike. When my parents reached him, they knew he needed to go to the hospital—the cut on his leg was very deep. The last thing my brother wanted was to go to the hospital. He kept crying, "Mom, make the pain go away!" My parents explained that if they left his leg to heal on its own, it would have a bad scar. But if they took him to the hospital, the doctors could help his wound to heal properly. They'd give him the special care he needed and make the pain go away. His wound would heal much faster.

Just like my brother needed a doctor to take care of his leg, we need to let Jesus take care of our inner wounds. It's important to remember that He already sees our whole situation *and* the solution.

Kathy, after you realized you had done something wrong, you immediately put up a barrier to shield yourself from the hurt and the guilt of that sin, instead of bringing it before Jesus, confessing it, and asking Him to cleanse you and give you the strength you need to go on. This may seem like the hardest thing to do—admitting that you're wrong—but in the end, you will walk away a clean and forgiven child of God, and that sure beats struggling in sin and guilt.

We can't always forget our mistakes. But we can learn from them and accept God's forgiveness. And then we're on the way to forgiving ourselves.

When I feel like I've really messed up and I'm feeling guilty and hurt, I go through these steps: First, I begin to share everything I'm feeling with the Lord and confess the things I've done wrong—every little detail. Second, I thank God for loving me and sending His Son, Jesus, so that I can be forgiven and have eternal life. I thank Him that nothing can take that away from me. Third, I take some words from my heart and put them to music.

I wrote this little poem once:

Walk by my side in all I do
so if I fall
I can reach for you.

I kept singing these words, like a song, over and over again. And guess what? The next morning, I felt better.

In fact, most of the time the system works so well that I fall asleep before I ever get to step number four: tell God what you're thankful for. The Lord cares so much for you and me. Although we make mistakes and disappoint Him, we can know His forgiveness and strength.

And we can also know his blessings.

It's Your Move

"Watch that move!"

"What move?"

"The most important move you'll ever make. The one right after you feel like you've really messed up your life."

"What are you talking about?"

"You can move in the direction of Jesus. His love mends the hurts. As you pray and listen, He'll direct your steps. Or you can let guilt slide in and tell you that you're a failure. You can move away from Jesus and shut Him out, along with everyone else. That's when you can lose your will to live."

"Why would anyone do *that?*"

"Because the pain we feel is so strong, sometimes it covers up any other feelings of love and understanding. But we should never forget God understands every hurt we bring to Him, even when we don't get the words right. There are no limits on God's love, His forgiveness, or His plan to make us everything He wants us to be. That's why Jesus said, 'I'll never leave you.'"

Chapter 7

SOMEONE TO WALK WITH US

Donalyn,

I've always been kind of quiet and kept a lot of my feelings to myself, so I'm not really comfortable writing about this. When I was in high school, my friends bullied me. Now that I'm a freshman in college, I thought it'd be over, but it isn't.

If I don't do something, they will continue to bully me, and I feel trapped. They don't listen when I try to explain what I want. They often try to make me feel ashamed. I have a boyfriend, but he treats me the same way, so no one understands me. Sometimes it gets so bad I want to run away, and I really don't care where I go.

Girls you think are your friends are the worst. I'd like things to be different, but I don't know what to do. I've made some new friends since I've been here, but it's hard for me to trust when I've been beaten so many times. Last week in my room, I took a bunch of pills I shouldn't have taken. I just wanted to go to sleep and not wake up, but I did wake up, and I had to face a new day with the same problems as yesterday. I'm tired and want a new life.

I am fighting just to be myself. I used to feel closer to God than I do now, but it seems like when I go to church, it's just words I hear the preacher say.

Sherrie

Dear Sherrie,

You may keep a lot of things to yourself, but being silent and allowing other people to bully you is not right. Stop listening to the lies you hear and try not to repeat them to yourself. When you feel ashamed or trapped, stand up for yourself. If they continue to bully you, simply walk away. If you don't hang out with them any longer, you may feel like you are missing out, but the truth is you don't need to be with them anyway.

People treat us the way we allow them to treat us. It's time you start being honest with yourself and with your friends. You will be so much happier if you speak up about what you need. If someone starts to bully you, look him or her in the eye and tell him to stop. If you are still being bullied, stay away from that person and report him to an adult you trust. If someone wants you to do something you know isn't right, stand up for yourself and say no. If someone doesn't like you because you said no, you don't need him or her in your life; it's that simple.

I know you might believe if you tell an adult, the bulling will get worse. Yes, it could, but you will now have someone supporting you, and you will not feel so alone. Every change we go through begins with little steps, and as you make these small changes, you will find a new strength in yourself that will make you feel better about who you are and what you want to do.

I believe in you, and I want you to begin to believe in yourself and in who you want to be. You won't have to stand behind a lie because there will be no reason for you to lie when you stand up to your friends.

Christ has never left your side—even though you don't feel very close to Him right now. How can you change this? Begin by being honest with God. Tell him you don't feel close to Him but you want to change how you feel. Ask Him to show you what you need to change in your own life to make this happen. God already knows how you feel, but He wants you to share your feelings with Him. This is the first step toward healing and restoration in your faith. Praying to God is our communication with Him. Talking with God, even about things that we may be ashamed of, brings us closer to Him and makes Him more real in our lives.

I have to mention your boyfriend because there is never a reason for a boyfriend not to treat you like a young lady. If you had a daughter, would you want her to stay in a relationship when the young man wasn't treating her very well? God doesn't want you with someone who isn't good to you. The longer you stay with him only takes away the time you could be with someone who is the kind of young man you should be with.

I think it's time to be honest and share your relationship with your parents. Your parents will give you the support you need to break away from a relationship that will only bring you pain the longer you stay with him. So often in a relationship, the boyfriend or girlfriend makes the other person feel responsible for his or her happiness, but you can't be responsible for someone's life. Right now, the most important thing you can do is be the best you you can be and take care of you. This is not a selfish attitude but a healthy one.

You can be kind and strong all at the same time. I praise God you are still here because I'm certain He has a special job only you can fulfill.

Trust Him, even if you have stepped away, because He is right there waiting for you.

God Bless You,
Donalyn

Dear Donalyn,

I was born with a blood disease that's kept me in and out of hospitals all my life. My parents are good to me, but I've always felt like a burden to my whole family.

Dad works hard so there'll be money for my medication and treatments. The bills are heavy-duty. Mom stays home so she'll be around if I need her. My brothers are terrific—they stop by my room after school and tell me about their day and what's going on with my friends. But they're also a constant reminder that I'm not like them. While they're working out for football season, my "workout" is another boring walk up and down a hospital hallway. They make plans with their girlfriends, but I wonder if I'll ever even have a date.

I'm sixteen now. I've watched my family rearrange their lives for me. They've given up so much. And there's nothing I can give *them*. I can't even promise to get well enough to one day plan and go on a vacation together. I don't know if I'll *ever* get well. I can't stand the way I'm ruining their lives.

I go through periods of remission that can last a couple of months. I feel much stronger and can do some of the things I really enjoy, like riding my bike and roller skating. I even go to school and go out for pizza with my friends. I feel like I'm alive. When I'm feeling good, I want to do everything I can because I don't know how long it will last. When I least expect it, my strength leaves. I'm left with only a memory of what it felt like to be like my brothers, *normal.*

It's hard to begin to feel like a real person—like an average guy—and then have it all taken away from you. Mom always tells me one day I'll be well. I ask her when that day will come. She can't tell me. Sometimes I pretend that I'm someone else and that I can do all the things I dream of. For a while, I feel better. But something always happens to remind me of who I really am.

A couple weeks ago, Mom went out for a few hours. While she was gone, I took an overdose of my medication. I was so tired; I just wanted to die. But my attempt only landed me in the hospital again, and afterward, I felt like I was a *greater* burden on my family. Mom blamed herself and said it was her fault because she left me alone. I didn't try to kill myself to hurt her! I'm just so sick of living this way.

I see two worlds. In one, everyone is healthy and alive and dreams come true. But the other? It's my world, a world where I'm just a burden to everyone. I don't want to live in my world anymore. Please tell me how I can live in my brothers' world.

Tommy

What's Your Name?
"I'm all alone."
"No you're not!"
"But I feel all alone."
"That's only because you want to feel alone."
"Then *you* tell me, where is everybody when I need them?"
"*I'm* here."
"What's your name?"
"Jesus."

Dear Tommy,

I can understand how you feel—alone in your private world. None of us wants to deal with being sick and feeling helpless. But *walling* yourself in your own world will only keep you from seeing your life is as worthwhile as your brothers'. We all live in the *same* world—the one God created—but we experience life differently. That's what makes us unique.

I think you know how much your family loves you. Remember that you're the only one who can separate yourself from them. Everyone has a special place inside himself where he can run and hide when he's hurting. But there's a danger of wanting to stay there forever. And you know what? I've never known a burden that gets better when you stuff it inside. Your family may not always understand—they're not walking in your tennis shoes. It's up to you to let them know how you feel.

There *is* hope. No matter what we face, for however long we live, someone will walk with us: *Jesus.* All of us have had at least one dream that will never come true because it requires us to change something we have no power to change. And it really does hurt to want something so badly when deep in your heart you know it will never come true.

Tommy, I want you to know something. I understand your pain because I spent eight years in and out of hospitals, too. At that time, I couldn't understand what purpose God could ever have for my life. Just like you, I got tired and was sick of the whole thing. Every time I faced another needle or thermometer or operation, I wanted to die. I asked the Lord if I could be in heaven with Him. When we are tired, our bodies and our minds are the most vulnerable.

I can't tell you how many nights my mom sat by my bed and told me, "When God takes something away, he gives you something else in return." I wondered what God would give me. You wonder if you will ever have a date. Girls often daydream about whom they'll fall in love with and marry one day. I wondered if a guy would ever care for a girl like me. By the time I was nineteen, I questioned if I would ever get well, and I already knew that I could never have a child.

But I had a very special dream. I wanted to be an artist and a writer. Many people encouraged me to do something with the talents God gave me, but I always had an excuse that never took my work further than my bedroom.

One night I had a dream that I died and went to heaven. My hands were empty; I had nothing to offer Him. I met the Lord, and He asked me, "What did you do with everything I gave you?"

That dream haunted me for a long time. I knew that I didn't want to meet the Lord empty-handed. I'd spent years telling myself that I wasn't worth much. What could I possibly have to give? In my eyes, I found no purpose for my life because I'd forgotten what I was worth to God.

What He began to teach me, I'll never forget. For the next several weeks, everything I heard seemed to have something to do with what we are worth as a person. I saw television shows about young people who couldn't walk but accomplished outstanding goals. I heard sermons about how much we're treasured by God. I was reminded that my life was worth Jesus dying on the cross. Then I heard someone say, "Everyone says it's so hard to get started. But all you have to do is begin." How could I begin?

I was the only one who could change. But things didn't start to change until I asked the Lord to help me know what it was He wanted me to do with my life. I should have known His answer. With an open heart, I listened to His Word by reading my Bible. I knew He wanted me to love Him above everything else so that He could direct my life and prepare me for what He wanted me to do—even when I didn't think I could do or give anything worthwhile.

The Lord had grabbed my attention! I finally let go of some of the dreams I knew could never come true. I stopped reminding myself of what I *couldn't* do, and I began to focus on what I *could* do.

One night, I announced to my family that I was going to go to college. This was a big surprise for everyone. Even so, I still went out and enrolled in a local college as an art student. I started out taking one class, and when I saw that I could complete one class, I took another. It wasn't long before I became a full-time student. I started by setting one goal and reaching it one step at a time. There were times when I had to drop a class because of my illness, but I always went back and picked up where I left off. I was older than most of the other students, and even though it was difficult, I never quit. *I graduated.* Starting with one small goal led me to accomplish a greater goal.

During those years, I finally did get well. Sometimes I feel guilty when I think of the days I wasted. But the Lord reminds me of the lessons I've learned, and I thank Him for bringing me this far.

In my heart, I continued to feel that the Lord wanted me to give my talents to Him. I knew I wanted to be a writer, so I plunged into my art and my writing. I gave my first book to the Lord, and I knew that if this was what He wanted from me, He would open a door. With a trembling heart, I sent my manuscript to a publisher. The Lord blessed that timid step, and it was accepted for publication! Finally, I knew something of what the Lord was giving me in return.

Tommy, the Lord also has a job for *you* to do. No one else can do it. It could be related to something you are involved with right now. Think about setting a small goal, and perhaps it can lead you to accomplish an even greater goal. *Trust* God—even when you can't imagine what purpose He has for your life. I know he can be trusted because He used me when I thought, like you, that I had nothing to give.

The Nicest Thing about You Is . . .

I used to worry about looking funny
and having people stare at me all day long.
I've even asked myself, "What am I doing here?"
Sure, I'm different.
But if God wanted me like everybody else,
He would have made me that way.
And besides, I've got a great personality.
Go ahead. We've all felt rejection
sometime in our lives.
A smile and a few more steps will get you in.
"But what if it doesn't? What if they don't
like me?"
You're never a failure when you try.
Anyway, it's hard to turn down a smile.

Chapter 8

GIVEN A SECOND CHANCE

She would give anything to change the moment that changed her life forever, but the truth was, she couldn't change one thing; it was too late. April was mad at herself for being so stupid, and on top of everything else, she couldn't make up her mind over one simple decision.

She woke to a new day and nothing had changed as she had hoped. She had the same choices facing her each day. Today, she thought she had no other choice but to pretend everything was all right. Then she made a new plan because she started to believe the lies she was telling herself. If she killed herself, her death would take care of everything.

She was so wrapped up in her own tears and pain she didn't answer her mother's call as she fought to get ready for school.

Her mother's frustration mounted as she entered into April's room. The young girl couldn't face her mother; she needed time to hide the pills under her pillow.

The mother placed her hand on her daughter's shoulder, and as she did, she caught a glimpse of the pills her daughter thought she was hiding.

Stunned, April's mother tried to act calm. "I came to check on you. You need to come down for breakfast."

Still, her daughter did not answer.

"Why are you so upset? There isn't anything we can't talk about."

April sat up and faced her mother. "Mom, I don't think you would understand, and I can't talk about it—not right now anyway."

"I can help you if you will let me," her mother said, not knowing what to say. "I can help you work through this. I hate seeing you hurt. Let's go downstairs for breakfast and start this day a little differently." April ran her hands across her eyes and followed her mom downstairs.

"I have enough time to drive you to school," her mother offered.

April forced a smile on her face, but in truth, if she had her way, she would be upstairs in a pill-induced coma.

April spent the day pretending everything was fine, and when school was over, she felt a little better about going to the football game. She never missed a game. She knew if she didn't go, her cell phone would blow up with too many questions, followed by more lies she didn't want to tell.

Lancer High School was right in the center of town, and there were no secrets in Belhaven, North Carolina, a consequence of living in a small country town where everyone knows your name and your life is an open book. For April it was home; it's where she grew up; it's what she knew; and she had no intentions of ever leaving, at least not until now.

She was certain of one thing: she'd never allow her family to endure small-town gossip; this was the least she could do to make things right.

"Hey, April, where have you been?" Amy asked as she opened the locker next to April's.

"I'm just slow today," April, said.

"Can you get your locker open?" Amy asked.

"No, I can't. I don't know what's wrong with me," April said, frustrated.

April held the lock in her hand, turning the inside dial and hoping she'd get it open this time.

"This is a first. You're usually at your locker before me and on the bus already."

"I'm far from perfect!" April replied with a snap in her voice.

"I didn't mean it that way," Amy said. "I've got to pick up the pompoms. I'll see you on the bus."

"Okay."

After watching her friend walk away, April focused on what she was doing, turned the dial one more time, and jerked the lock from the handle, finally opening her locker door. She tried to ignore her refection in the mirror attached inside her locker, but it was staring back at her, bigger than life. She had no other choice but to look at herself. There was a time she had a daily habit of making sure everything about her appearance looked just right, but today was different.

She didn't want to see her reflection. The mirror reflected too many memories, memories she wanted to forget. On the first day of high school, her father was determined to accompany her and bring along a mirror to hang in her locker.

"Dad, are you serious? I mean, really? You're going into school with me and carrying that mirror to hang in my locker?" April was hoping he would understand how embarrassed she would be.

She could handle the first day of high school without him, but she knew he wasn't going to change his mind. When they pulled into the school parking lot and she saw so many freshman students standing on the sidewalk with a parent and a mirror in their arms, her worst nightmares went away. She was actually happy he was with her, but her pride would never tell him so.

He carefully hung the mirror in her locker, and when the bell rang, he gave her a big, daddy hug and sent her off for the day. Even today she could hear him say, "This mirror will remind you of how beautiful you are to me."

"Daddy, will I still be beautiful to you now?" she whispered.

"Hey, April, come on! The bus is leaving," a voice yelled across the hall. He was right. The bus wouldn't wait, and if she was going, she needed to stop feeling sorry for herself and follow her friends. If they paid attention, they would have noticed there wasn't the usual bounce in her step or bubbly excitement she usually showed before a game.

Today the football game wasn't the most important thing on her mind. What she really wanted was to be left alone and hide from the rest of the world. She knew she had to keep with the plan. Taking a deep breath, she lifted her head, pulled her shoulders back, and headed for the school parking lot. Climbing on the bus, she was happy there wasn't an empty seat with her friends. Lifting her backpack, she slipped in a lonely front seat near the driver.

It wasn't long before the bus came to a complete stop and the driver pulled a long handle, opening the door. A stream of students pushed around her, but April raised herself up and held onto the rails while everyone raced past her. Walking onto the field, she told herself she would give 100 percent tonight, cheering her team on to victory. This could be her last game, and she wanted to lift her head high and walk off that field knowing she did her best. This was the one thing in her life she had control of. She could do this, no problem. Today she had learned she could pretend by putting on a smile; it was the mask she could wear for the world to see—until she was ready to share the truth, and she really didn't know when that would be.

Catching up with the rest of the cheerleaders, she stepped right in line as they began to practice some of the cheers before the game. Looking around, she knew she was in the midst of a thousand people, yet she felt completely alone. As hard as she tried, she couldn't let go of what was digging into her heart. If she shared her secret, what would her friends say, and what would they say behind her back? Those thoughts kept her silent. It was too late for advice, and no one could be as hard on her as she had already been on herself.

The same questions played over and over again in her head like a never-ending song: *Why didn't I wait? I've hurt so many people, but most of all . . .* She couldn't bring herself to say—or even think—the words.

The next two hours passed quickly. When the game was over, her team had won, and everyone broke out in celebration.

"Tommy, cut it out!" April yelled.

"What's wrong with you?"

"I don't want my hair full of confetti; that's all!" she yelled.

April picked up her bag and started walking off the field. "Where are you going?" two other cheerleaders yelled.

"My parents are waiting for me; I've got to run!" she yelled back.

She was never late, and she wasn't going to start tonight. She was completely and emotionally drained. April was ready to go home, hide under the covers of her bed, and pray she'd wake to a totally different life with different results and a different future. She remembered the pills she had hidden under her pillow. Taking her life didn't seem as urgent as it had this morning, not now that she had gotten through what she thought would be the hardest day of her life.

April slid into the back seat of her parents' car and let out a long breath as if she had just run a race and it was over now.

"We'll be home soon. Are you feeling all right?" her mother asked.

"I'm fine, Mom. It's just been a long day at school, and I'm tired."

April couldn't help but wonder how long she could keep her secret. She was certain she didn't have much time before her parents would notice the change in her, and they would be right.

"I hope you had a better day at school."

"I did," April answered softly.

She didn't want to talk, not tonight, at least not until she could answer the questions that haunted her for the last twenty-four hours. How would she tell them? She feared their disappointment would be more than she could handle. She felt like she had blown her life, but the thoughts of disappointing her parents made it even worse.

Will they ever forgive me? she wondered.

From the back seat, April stared at her parents—her loving, devoted parents. They trusted her, and they loved her. *How will I ever tell them?* The voice in her heart tried to make sense of it all, but her soul was broken. *We didn't plan this. I don't know how it happened; it just did. It wasn't supposed to be like this; I'm too young.*

The anger inside of her started to surface as they pulled into their driveway. April picked up her backpack, and without a word to her parents, she entered her room and shut the door. She wanted to stop thinking and turn off the voices in her head. She raised her hands and pressed hard against her temples, but it was useless. She was no more able to quiet her thoughts than to go back in time and relive her life. She reached for the pills under her pillow, and as she did, she felt this sick feeling come over her. The pills were not there.

"Okay, I got it. It's not just about me anymore; it's about you too, but I don't know if I can handle you. I'm only sixteen," April said aloud.

For a split second, April felt as if the baby inside of her had a voice, and she could hear what the baby was saying: *Give me a chance to love you back, and I promise we will go through this together.* April paused for a moment. She suddenly realized taking her life would also kill her child, and it frightened her so much she started to cry.

April's mom came into her room and saw the tears in her daughter's eyes. "April, what are you doing?" her mother asked. "Let's talk about this. What could be so bad that you want to take these pills?" Her mother held the missing pills in her hand.

"I took these pills from under your pillow after I came home this morning. If you take your life, the Lord would need to take my life too. Something is really hurting you, and I need to know what it is."

"Mom, I don't know if I can talk about it right now."

"I want you to understand something. When you become a mother and your child is hurting, you would move heaven and earth to make things better. As long as you see your child hurting, you will hurt too. God's love for us is like that. When he sees his children hurting, He wants us to bring our problems to Him and to trust Him to take care of us through the storms and pains in our lives."

"But, will He forgive us?"

"Yes, He will forgive us—if we ask Him to."

"Mom, I do understand, more than you know." April lowered her head and began to cry.

"April, I love you, and you will always be my heart, but I can't help you unless you tell me what's hurting you."

"Mom, I'm hurting because I've done something that will hurt you and Dad, and I don't know how to tell you."

"There is nothing you could do to keep us from loving you. If you were to take your own life, the pain of losing you would never go away, and I would never forgive myself because I would wonder what I could have done to save you. Please tell me what's wrong. We can work this out together."

"Mom, I'm so sorry." April could hardly say the words. "I'm pregnant." April leaned into her mother and cried.

"April, look at me." April's mother turned her daughter's face toward hers. "Oh honey, if I lost you and this baby you carry, my pain would be so much greater than what you are feeling right now. We will work this out together as a family, and that is the only answer you need for now. Taking your life would never be the answer."

April could hardly believe her mother's words. "Do you forgive me?" she asked.

"April, your timing isn't the greatest, but you are my daughter, and your father and I will stand beside you all the way. You are not alone."

April was crying even harder now. Her mother continued, "I love you. I'm sorry you didn't feel like you could come to me right away and tell me what was wrong. I've been worried sick since I saw you with the bottle of pills this morning. I spent my morning praying for you. God has answered my prayer, and in time, there will be lessons in this experience He will teach all of us. I love you." Her mother's words were honest and strong.

"I love you, Mama." April said.

Chapter 9

OPEN ARMS

D ear Donalyn,
   I wasn't happy. I wasn't *any*thing. I used to be really wild and do things that I don't even want to talk about now. The friends I used to hang around with would have wild parties, and all of us had sex with the guys we liked. I was raised in a home where we went to church. But there wasn't very much talk about the kind of life God wanted us to lead.

My parents got a divorce last year, and I really started to get confused about what was right and wrong. Mom was so busy working after Dad left, she didn't keep up with what my older sister and I were doing. My sister got involved with drugs, and I really didn't care about who I went with. I felt so lost. I'd pray, but it didn't change me. My sister was stoned most of the time, and I started to feel like I had to look after her. So I stopped running around with my friends as much as I used to. The crazy thing about all of this was our parents didn't even notice.

One night, when I was changing the channels on my radio, I heard a girl talking about drugs. I kept it there and found out she'd been a prostitute and a drug addict. Then one day, someone told her about Jesus and that He wouldn't give up on her. He told her that Jesus would love her in a way that would fill all her needs; He would give her the strength to give up dope and the confidence in herself to find a job. She accepted the Lord, and she's married now and a mother.

In the past, when I listened to Christian radio stations, I laughed at some of the preachers—but now I couldn't learn enough about Jesus. One night, I heard a sermon about knowing you're saved. I started crying, and I knew what Jesus was trying to tell me. I accepted Jesus as my personal Savior that night. I asked Him to live in my heart and take charge of my life.

It wasn't easy for me, going to school and seeing my friends. They knew I was different, but they still wanted me to do some of the things I used to do with them. But, I didn't. I also thought I could talk to my family about Jesus, but they really didn't want to hear it. My boyfriend really didn't understand either. I told him that Jesus had changed my life, and I wanted to start doing what was right for me. I still wanted to see him, but I didn't want us to have sex anymore. For the first time in my life, I felt clean.

But then my sister told me I needed help, and I watched my friends walk out of my life. The boyfriend I didn't think I could live without broke up with me.

The more I read my Bible, the more I wanted to be with Jesus. I felt all alone, and I cried and prayed. I couldn't go on any longer. I thought it would be better to be in heaven with Jesus than here on earth. So I cut my wrists and lay down on my bed. I woke up later in a hospital bed. My sister told me she found me just in time to save my life. My first thought was, *Why didn't she let me die?*

After I got home, I had a lot of time to think about what I'd done. I still felt alone, but I realized the Lord didn't want me to die. Sometimes I get scared because I wonder if I'll ever try it again.

Heather

> Choose friends who have the qualities
> of love
> and happiness
> because those things are contagious.

Dear Heather,

When we're unhappy, it keeps us from feeling all the good things in life. It makes us forget that we can have good feelings inside us again, that those good feelings are within our grasp—if we choose to reach for them. Being unhappy for a long time is a real downer. It can keep you from seeing bright tomorrows or feeling strong enough to try hard at anything you do.

When you go through problems and keep falling down, you need to share with someone you trust and respect. Do you have a friend like that? If you don't feel comfortable sharing with someone your own age, talk to a professional counselor. Seeking help doesn't mean you're weird or anything like that. It means something is *right*. You're growing as a person, and you care enough about yourself to say, "I need someone to help me."

I want you to remember something else: There's one Counselor who's always there for you. And when you ask Him to help, no problem is too big or too small because He cares about every detail of your life. Jesus' tender mercy and loving-kindness is eternal. He has unfailing love for everyone who calls upon His name.

We often forget God waits for us with open arms. On days when I feel alone, I ask the Lord to wrap His arms around me so that I can feel His love. I once learned that when I bring my needs to the Lord in the morning, then He stays with me all through the day. When I ask for help, He always answers my prayers and wraps me up with so much love that I'm bursting with it. I can *feel* the joy that comes with the love of our Lord. Guess what happens next? This love gives you an inner confidence so that you can believe in yourself and get through whatever you're facing.

He'll do all this for you, too, when you pray and ask for His help. Now, that doesn't mean that everything will turn out the way *we* want.

In your mind, it was right for your parents to stay together. When you love your parents, it's hard to understand why they can't love each other. I believe that every parent who is going through a divorce would do anything to keep his child from hurting. But the parent's own hurt is so strong he doesn't know *how* to keep you from hurting.

But even what we *know* is right doesn't always happen. At this point, I'll bet it appears that nothing lasts forever, so doing what seems right doesn't seem to matter that much anymore. These are the times we need to pray for our families. We must ask God to help us accept and understand the decisions of others, especially the decisions that affect our lives. When we put our faith in others, we will always be disappointed. People aren't perfect, so they continue to make mistakes. That's why we should *pray* for those we love, but *look* to God and His truths as our perfect example.

Heather, when you wanted someone—a *person*—to care for you, your boyfriend was wrapped up in the addiction of sex. That sounds cold and uncaring, but sex can be just as strong an addiction as a drug. An immature sexual relationship has little concern for one's deep personal feelings or beliefs. The freedom to be yourself in the relationship is lost. You feel as though you're tied up in an emotional cage. You thought you would feel loved, but instead, you still feel incomplete.

When God told us to wait for sex until marriage, it wasn't because He wanted to hurt us. It was because He wanted to keep us from *being* hurt. Today, young people across the world are learning in some pretty sad ways about the dangers of sex outside of marriage.

As we grow up, each of us is confronted with a very important question: "What kind of life am I going to live?" No one else is responsible for how *you* answer that question, of how you live. Only you are.

But the fact of the matter is, you can *want* to do the right thing and keep failing. Your behavior won't change until you change the desires in your heart. And how do you do that? By asking the Lord to come into your life. Through your love for Jesus, your desire will be to become the kind of person He wants you to be.

The night you accepted Jesus as your personal Savior, you took the first step. And as you grow in the Lord, you'll better understand everything that God is and will be in your life.

Breaking up with a boyfriend who didn't understand where you're coming from is a smart move. God also understands your need for friendships. Pray that He'll bring Christian friends into your life, ones who'll help you grow in the Lord.

Feeling clean for the first time in your life was God's grace and forgiveness. After what you've been through, you now know God's cleansing and His love. Let that be your strength in standing up to temptations. Each day you'll grow stronger in the Lord, and what's right will seem important again. The respect for yourself and what you want out of life will be so clear that decisions won't be as hard to make.

God doesn't want you to dwell on the problems of the past. He wants you to make *today* count. Even though you will still make mistakes, you can be thankful for God's special grace in forgiving your goof-ups.

We need to forgive ourselves for the past. You need to forgive yourself for all the things you've done. Until you ask for God's forgiveness and accept it as a free gift, you'll never be able to forgive yourself or understand what living a joy-filled life is all about.

You need to forgive your mom and dad for getting a divorce and also to forgive your older sister for not being able to be there for you when you needed someone. Your sister has yet to understand how God has changed your life. In time, she'll see the example that you can be for Christ in your own home. Instead of thinking you need help, she'll want to know more about the difference God has made in your life. Sure, things won't always be easy. But God can give meaning and purpose to all you are and everything you do.

When I was a kid, I was running down the sidewalk one day after school and *splat!* I almost knocked down a grown man twice my size. As he grabbed me, I was glad to hear him laughing and to see that it was my minister, not some stranger who was going to be mad at me for not watching where I was going.

He also surprised me with these words, "When you're unhappy, it shows all over your face."

How did he know that I had a lot on my mind? I wondered. I asked him, "Do you think I have an unhappy face?"

"Yes, I do."

He was right. And it wasn't long before I was spilling out some of the things that were going on in my life. After we'd talked for a while, he asked, "Donalyn, what do you think God meant when He said He wanted us to have an *abundant* life?"

That very moment, I could feel a smile creep across my face. Without hesitation, I answered, "He wanted us to have the good things in life."

"And do you have that in your life right now?" My answer had to be no.

Later, when I was a little older, I first realized that I'm the only one responsible for *who* I am and what I'm *doing*. The realization hit me hard. I knew I had a lifetime of choices I had to make.

Heather, you've been through a great deal at a young age, and so many of the things you were involved in made you unhappy. When you accepted Jesus into your life and all your so-called friends took off, it was only natural that you felt alone. You thought heaven would be so much better—and it will be! But God has timed your life. Don't take away from Him the gifts you can give Him by living as a lighted candle in a dark world. The Lord doesn't want you to take your life. His arms are reaching for you—to give you encouragement and a full, happy life.

At this moment, I am holding you next to my heart. When you get discouraged, remember how important you are to the Lord. As you grow with Him and learn to believe in yourself, the fear that you'll take your own life will fade and finally pass away. Instead, you'll be more concerned about not having enough hours in the day to do all the things you want to do.

The Lord has put you in a place where He can use you the most. The story you heard on the radio about the girl who was a prostitute and drug addict is an example of how important it is to talk about what the Lord has done for you. For your friends and family, your life may be the only example they'll ever see of the difference God can make in a person's life. Share God's love and continue to read His Word so you'll know His truths and His answers for you.

What greater joy can there be than to meet the Lord knowing that you fulfilled His purpose for your life?

Where Are You Going?

"Hey, Scarecrow. You look like you could use a workout."

"If you think I'm in rough shape, take a look at yourself. You don't look very happy. What's wrong?"

"Nothing ever turns out right for me. I can't seem to do anything right."

"You can do things you never thought you could do, if you *believe in yourself.* A long time ago, nations would choose a soldier to fight in their place. One nation chose a giant, but the other nation knew of no one who would face the giant. A young, inexperienced boy believed that he could beat the giant. He prayed, asking God to give him the courage he needed to fight the giant. With God's help, and believing in himself, he beat the giant. And his nation won . . . Hey, where are you going?"

"I can't hang around here. I've got things to do!"

Chapter 10

A Mother's Prayer

Dear Lord,

It's me again—Mary. I know for the last two days it seems as though every breath I've taken has been in prayer to you. I'm so confused. I thought if I came and prayed in this chapel, I would feel your presence closer to me. How I need you to fill me with your strength.

I'd give anything to wake from this nightmare and find out it was only a dream. Then all three of my children would be with me, and Robert wouldn't be in this hospital, dying. Lord, what amount of suffering caused him to try and hang himself? Why didn't I *know* the pain he was going through? Why couldn't I have been there to stop him? Now I feel dead inside.

What was I to do? He was my son, and I didn't want him to suffer any more. The doctors told me he was brain dead, his lungs had collapsed, and he was bleeding internally. Only the respirator was keeping him alive. How long could I let him live like that? My heart was breaking. What could I do?

But when I have to face his younger brother and sister—I don't know what I'll say to them. They're only children. They don't understand what's happened. *I* don't understand. How can I help them struggle through their pain, when I don't know how to bear my *own*?

Lord, you are my only hope. Pour your words into my heart so I'll know what to say to them. Give me the strength I need to hold us together as a family.

The day Robert was born, I thanked you for giving me a beautiful son. I can still feel the joy I felt the first time I held "my Bobby" in my arms. Now, I've given him back to you. He's been a good boy, and I know you love him. All my children are in your hands.

So am I.

------- ᴋᴥ -------

Robert committed suicide July 31, 1985.
He was taken off the respirator August 2, at 8:15 a.m.
and died at 10:30 a.m. the same day.

Bobby's Memory

When he was only nine years old, I pretended not to see him place the card on his swing. I remember the tears that fell as I read his words, "Mom, thanks for loving me."

As He was growing up, if he could only have remembered to replace the pain with the *love*, he would have chosen to live. He would be with me today.

Chapter 11

IN THE MIDDLE

Dear Donalyn,

My brother Keith was a troubled child ever since I can remember. When he was little, he threw terrible, long temper tantrums. Nobody could get near him. These continued until he was nine or ten and then finally subsided. But his internal anguish took on other forms. Sometimes he would refuse to go to school. He would even threaten to kill himself with a steak knife at the dinner table.

When Keith was seventeen, he moved into a boarding house. He worked at a veterinary clinic and planned to go to college and med school when he finished high school. Four months before graduation, he was taken into police custody when he unknowingly accompanied a friend on a burglary. When the police phoned my mom to tell her, she blew up and refused to go see him. The minute she hung up, I knew she wanted to kick herself.

But I couldn't turn my back on him. I drove an hour into town and took Keith to a coffee shop to talk. I insisted he go and talk to Mom. That was a big mistake. I treated him as if he had no other choice than to go see her. In his mind, she'd caused him a lifetime of problems.

Three long hours we sat at Mom's house, listening to her apologize for everything from pinning his diapers wrong to having divorced Keith's dad, to not knowing his real needs. She was in tears, pleading for another chance. Keith sat across the room with his back turned, stone cold and silent.

I got frustrated. I tried to "muscle him." "You don't have to forgive her or *love* her," I said, "but you *will*, this weekend, move back home and live under this roof until you finish high school. Then you won't have to support yourself. You can save money and move out the day you graduate."

That was on a Wednesday night. On Saturday afternoon, the day before he was due to move back home—at least according to my "divine plan"—Mom had *another* change of heart.

"If Keith is that miserable with me, I'll not only let him live away from home, I'll *pay* his rent. Please call and tell him that for me."

Keith never got the phone call. At seven o'clock that night, I tried to call Mom. Keith was dead. His body had been found in an alley near a local department store. I became frantic when Mom didn't answer her phone or door. I was so afraid that Keith had murdered Mom, then killed himself. He hated her that much.

When I found Mom, she was okay—at least physically. But Keith's death had left her with more hurt than he'll ever know. We found out he had jumped off a parking garage, directly across the street from the hospital where he'd been born. His birth certificate was in his pocket. He had circled the blank spot where his father's name should have gone. (Mom's marriage to Keith's dad was annulled before his birth.) A search of his pockets also revealed a suicide note: "I have no father. I am a bastard."

That piece of paper is all Mom and I have left of Keith—except our guilt.

Love,
Kelly

Suicide
He's Dead.

Dear Kelly,

It isn't easy being in the middle, is it? Or to find ways to mend relationships—especially in a family. It's a heavy burden for anyone to carry, especially when it involves people you love. And when your brother took his own life, nothing was settled. You feel you'll always remain in the middle.

How do you move forward when everything has stopped? That's a hard question. But you can begin by trying to understand.

Your mother's anger and her refusal to see your brother was her first reaction to the shocking news that he was in trouble with the police. I think you know that she wouldn't have let him stay in jail. But you saw yourself as the only one who could help him. It never seems to work when we think we're responsible for someone else's life. Making excuses for the behavior of others never changes anything, nor does it help them.

We can *be there* for them—willing to love and understand them—but they have to take the responsibility for their own life, or they'll never learn to take care of themselves.

It seems obvious to me that your brother had a mind of his own. You shouldn't feel guilty because you encouraged him to go home and talk with your mother. You had no way of knowing, and perhaps he didn't either, what the outcome would be.

Because Keith was unable to handle his own feelings, it seems to me he was very good at letting everyone else feel guilty. Your mother spent hours apologizing for almost everything she had done "wrong" in her life. Maybe this continued to encourage Keith to feel that everything wrong in his life was her fault. Sitting across the room, stone cold and with his back turned to your mother, was his way of saying, "You hurt me, so I'll hurt you."

What I'm saying may seem very cold, but it's not meant to be that way. Keith had lost control of his feelings and his behavior. He didn't know how to put together the pieces of his own life, and he was hurting so much that he lashed out in pain. His reactions hurt not only him but everyone around him. If he had a choice, he wouldn't have wanted things to be this way.

At an early age, your brother began to show signs of not being able to handle his emotions. Not knowing how to properly express his feelings, he allowed his emotions to run wild. Many people have to deal with a problem just like your brother's every day. Through professional help, they begin recognizing their behavior patterns. They learn to calm down the moment they begin to feel uncontrollable outbursts of emotion.

When we're able to look at a situation calmly, we can better understand and accept the situation. Then we can make the correct decision and behave accordingly. In time, you're able to exchange an unacceptable learned behavior for a proper response to your emotions. No longer do these outbursts control your behavior. Once you've learned to control your behavior, you're able to have better relationships with others and live a full and productive life.

I can understand your working so hard to try and make things better in your home; and even though things didn't work out the way you would have wanted them to, you have no reason to feel guilty. How would you have felt if you had done nothing at all?

Guilt makes you feel so helpless. You want to turn back the clock. You want to do things differently. The "if only'" can go on forever. Guilt is just another burden, and God's Word tells us to bring our burdens to Him. When we feel guilty, for whatever reason, we should remember to give our feelings to the Lord and ask Him to help us forgive ourselves and allow Him to heal our broken heart. Focusing attention on the past, we'll never be able to give today and tomorrow all that we have.

Keith's decision to take his own life was his. The note he left was a cry of pain. Keith wasn't a "bastard"; he was a young man who was hurting, and he didn't know how else to express his pain. I'm thankful that our heavenly Father understands pain. God comforts the brokenhearted, and His understanding goes beyond our own. God also knows the pain you and your mother are feeling. He has always been there waiting for you. Give Him your guilt and allow Him to help bear your anguish.

I cannot begin to explain why there is suffering in our world. It's a fact of life that no one is free from living through disappointments or experiencing great pain. I thank God that we do not have to experience this alone. I think the greatest pain of all would be not having Christ in our lives to share our burdens. What a blessing it is to know that there's not one thing in our lives that we have to carry alone.

We can let suffering end our lives or hold us back from living our life at its full potential. Because the love of the Lord is freely given, the choice is ours to make: move toward death or move toward life.

I've seen God use tragedy in the lives of others to prepare them for a greater ministry. And because of the pain they experienced, they were able to understand and help someone else who was hurting. Suffering can also give us a closer relationship with God as we learn to share everything with Him.

Kelly, I am certain that you have a deeper understanding of those who are hurting. You may have just the right words inside of you that will help someone else think twice before trying to take his own life. Let the Lord guide you in His direction and His purpose.

When you have a willing heart, God can use you to reach out to others when no one else can understand. I know if you ask Him to take this tragedy and turn it around for Him, He will. Wait and see.

Under Wraps

It's Christmas morning, and I just know I'm getting a model plane. It's the only present I've asked for all year. I told them the model I wanted, what store it was in, and how much it cost. There isn't any way they could have forgotten.

Where's my model plane? There were so many beautiful presents under the tree. How could one of them *not* be what I really wanted?

Then I heard a voice. "Here's another present with your name on it. Do you want to know what it is?"

"Father, does it matter what it is? I didn't get the one present I asked for."

"Don't let your disappointment keep you from opening a present that could hold something better that you ever dreamed of."

Chapter 12

THE PROMISE

*J*ake, wake up! It's me—Chris.

Chris, what are you doing here?

I came to help you.

Help me? With what?

Jake, don't play games with me. I know what's going on. I came back to stop you from committing suicide.

Why do you want to do that? *You* did it!

I didn't know what I was doing.

That's hard to believe. You planned every detail—from the letters you left to the gun you used to kill yourself.

Jake, listen—I'm trying to tell you I didn't know what I was doing! I was only seventeen. *I had my whole life in front of me. I made a mistake—a tragic mistake. And now I'm trying to keep you from making the same one.*

Chris, why *did* you kill yourself? You had everything going for you. You were the top player on our school hockey team. Everyone liked you. Good grades were a breeze for you. I wish they were as easy for me. Everything you did you always did well.

You know why, Jake? Because I tried to control every situation in my life. I had to do my best at everything, and I expected too much from others. When things didn't work out according to my perfect plan, it was hard for me to handle. I got so caught up with losing the first girl I thought I loved that I couldn't see any further than my own feelings of hurt and rejection. If I had only stopped to think about what I was doing, I would have realized that just because one relationship doesn't work out, it doesn't mean you'll never have another one.

And you know what else? I didn't think about my family or what it would do to my parents. I really didn't think about being dead — about the finality of it. I didn't have the perfect plan. Neither do you.

Jake, I can't stop you from killing yourself, but I beg you to think about what it would mean. I know how you feel deep down in your gut. I couldn't see anything in myself worth living for either. But you must make yourself see your life further than where you are right now. Give yourself a chance to get through your feelings of hurt and helplessness.

There is a perfect plan, a plan that brings hope and life and joy back again. But it's not in us. You don't have to earn it; you don't have to bear your feelings all by yourself. Other people care, and God cares. I know that now. God sees so much more in us than we see in ourselves.

I know that sounds really simple, but it's true. It's only when we climb out of our own problems and reach out to God and others around us that we receive the love and understanding that we all need.

Jake, it's time for me to go. Look — the rain has stopped. And there's a rainbow through the trees! Think about it. The rainbow reminds us of the promise from God that He will carry us through every mistake, every disappointment, and every tear — and He'll wipe them away with His love.

"Jake, wake up!"

"Mom?"

"I've been calling for you for the last ten minutes. Are you all right? You look pale."

"Yeah . . . Hey, Mom! Come over to my window and look at this rainbow. Isn't it great?"

"It's beautiful. Wish we could look at it all day, but there's a lot we have to do. I've got to get ready—and so do you. Breakfast in five minutes!"

"Hey, Chris—it's more than beautiful. It's a promise. I'm going to live."

Friends First

It took a broken relationship and time to teach me that a shattered heart does mend. It's not the end of the world if I don't have a date on Saturday night or if I never exchange class rings. Real love begins with *friendship,* and it's important to take it one day at a time.

On the Occasion of Chris's Memorial Service

I have just a few words to say to the people in this congregation. My fond hope is that they will somehow have an impact—on you and all those you touch.

You see before you a grieving parent who has suffered an irreplaceable loss. As I look around this room and remember what happened at our home, I feel all of your help, love, and support. Yet, in spite of it all, I am still struck by one thought. All this outpouring of love, all these generous gifts of time, affection, and genuine caring are so much appreciated—but none of it can bring back our Chris. We have to come to grips with the fact that he is gone from this earth. Forever.

And so I have a message I would like to leave with you, young people. I pray it will influence any of you who suffer from the same trouble and torment that Chris did that led him to take his own life.

It's this: If you or a friend is going through something that makes you feel desperate, that makes you consider doing what Chris did, then I ask you . . . I urge you . . . no, I *plead* with you to reach out to someone before you commit that final act.

Reach out to a friend. He will listen, understand, and help. Reach out to your family, in spite of what you think they will say. You'll find love and understanding from them and maybe even some way of handling your problem. And if all that fails, then for God's sake, reach out to a minister, a priest, a rabbi, or a counselor. There are thousands of them all over the United States who are ready, willing, and anxious to share God's love and a better sense of purpose than taking your own life.

I beg you—reach out!

Chris's Dad

Excerpted from a message delivered at Chris's memorial service at Dunwoody Methodist Church in Atlanta, Georgia.

Chapter 13

BURIED SECRETS

Dear Donalyn,

I was the one who found him. I thought maybe something was wrong when we were together the night before. Todd looked at me so funny when he kissed me. Then he said goodbye and drove away. I tried to call him all night long. I couldn't understand where he could be.

He had an apartment within walking distance from my dorm room on campus. I was so scared. He didn't tell me he was going anywhere. Why didn't he answer the phone?

The next morning really early, I ran over to his apartment and banged on the door. No one answered. When I reached for the door, I found it unlocked, so I walked in.

His bedroom door was shut. I knocked and yelled, "Todd, open the door!" But he didn't answer. I was really getting scared. I yelled again and kicked the door open.

And there he was. I'll never forget it. All that blood on those white sheets and on the floor. I wanted to scream, but I couldn't talk—it was like my voice and my legs and everything were frozen. I thought I should call the hospital, but I couldn't move.

Just then, Todd's brother walked in and saw the whole mess. He made me go sit in the living room. All I could hear were a bunch of fuzzy words that drifted in and out. Two other guys rushed in to help his brother carry Todd out.

But as they were carrying him, Todd groaned, and I'll never forget thinking, *He's alive!* Todd didn't want to go anywhere. He kicked one of the guys when they were putting him in the back seat of the car. I couldn't believe how strong he was, even after losing all that blood!

Someone else picked me up and took me to the hospital. I don't remember who. It was like being in a dream in slow motion.

When I got to the hospital, Todd's mom and dad were there. She screamed at me—as if it was all my fault. Over and over: "What did you *do* to him?"

So I ran away from the hospital, with all the ugly sights and sounds and smells and all the people's faces staring at me.

In the hospital, they put him in the psych ward. I couldn't see him or hear from him. After he'd been in the hospital for two months, they told me he was going home. I knew no one had cleaned up his room since the day he left. So I did. It took hours, but I cleaned up all the dried blood. I didn't want him to have to come back to that mess. It made me sick—actually sick—and I cried for a while.

Then I opened his closet. Any other time, Todd was a slob. But everything was neatly placed in bags—with people's names on them. All his clothes were washed and hung up. There was even a bag for me with a cassette tape in it, but I was too scared to to hear what he had to say.

That was when it hit me. Todd had *really wanted* to kill himself! How come I didn't know? Was I weird, or something, to have a boyfriend like that? I must be a real mess.

That's when I decided not to tell anyone about what happened. If I told anyone, they'd think Todd and I were both freaks. It was no problem keeping this a secret. Todd's parents covered it up, too. No one in school knew. They thought Todd had gotten real sick and had to stay home for a while.

But I can't cover up what's going on inside *me*. What's wrong with me? I keep crying. Inside, I keep wondering if it *is* my fault. What did I do that made him cut himself all over like that? How come I end up with the weird boyfriends?

Todd tried to kill himself a year ago today. I still feel like my stomach's being torn apart. But I'm scared to tell anybody— even you—because I'm afraid you'll think I'm stupid or weird.

Carmen

Why?

Why is it that some people fight to stay alive and others choose to die by their own hand?

Dear Carmen,

Being able to share what you've held inside for so long was the beginning of your healing. You will never *forget* those experiences, but you *can* get over them and go on with your life.

When you go through a traumatic experience, it's normal to feel as though you're going through it in a daze. Your reactions are slower because you're in a state of shock. I think it's our mind's way of getting us through that experience so we don't fall apart.

When you reached the hospital and Todd's mother screamed at you, it was just her way of denying that her son did not want to go on living. She blamed you needlessly. The shock and hurt she felt kept her from stopping long enough to try and understand what had happened or to take the time to talk with you. She was desperately trying to find someone to blame because of the deep pain she felt.

If you think back to the times in your own life when you've gotten upset, I'll bet you can recall saying things you really didn't mean. As we all do, I'll bet you've also directed your guilt or pain at someone else by blaming him. The person who says hurting words may get over it and not even remember what he said. But the person who *heard* them may continue to be upset for a long time. Hurting words, taken to your heart, can cause you to question yourself and feel insecure about your behavior.

We all need to remember that what we say can become a powerful weapon to hurt or to build. Offer words of understanding when others are going through a difficult time; try to bring people together. We need to lean on each other. It's so important that we ask the Lord to give us the right kind of hearts and the words to say when someone is hurting. The first step in working out problems is *always* going to God in prayer. God also has an answer for those of us that have *been* hurt by the actions of others. By asking Him to forgive those who have hurt us, He heals our hearts. The memory will always be there, but the pain won't be the same.

Time also heals our wounds, and it allows us some distance to look at what really happened. It gives us a chance to try to understand—you know, what *really* happened. Don't look for something you didn't do, just because someone shot blame in your direction. Don't let those words strip you of all your worth.

You're so close to the situation, Carmen—and you're feeling so bad about yourself—you can't see all the good others see in you right now. What a caring heart you have! You didn't just think about yourself. You went back to Todd's room. (I think it was also your way of trying to understand what had happened.)

And no, you're not weird. Todd isn't weird either. Todd was having a hard time coping with his own feelings. That doesn't mean, however, that in time he can't go on to live a full and happy life. Todd wasn't being honest about his feelings with himself or others around him. I bet if you asked Todd today, he would tell you it wasn't the right thing to do.

When we feel like giving up, it's hard to remember that these depressed feelings won't last forever. It's like having a huge pile of papers stacked on your desk. Then one day, you're looking for some papers you think you've lost. It isn't until you go through the papers stacked on your desk that you find what you were looking for. Our feelings can be just like that stack of papers. Sometimes sad feelings are stacked on top of the good feelings, and we have to really look in order to find the feelings of wanting to live—even though they've been there all along.

There was no way you could have known Todd was going to try and kill himself, unless he shared those feelings with you. When someone we're close to is going through a hard time, we may be aware that something's wrong, but we can't know what he is *thinking* unless he tells us.

I'm sorry that his parents wanted to hide what happened to him, because it made you feel like you had to hide *your* feelings. I'm so thankful we don't have to hide our feelings from God. We can come to Him with all our feelings, even when the words are too hard to say.

> At some point
> everyone
> needs
> someone
> to
> lean
> on.

Chapter 14

"DEAR FATHER . . ."

Dear Donalyn,

For sixteen years, I thought my dad was dead. Mom had made up a pretty good story, and I believed her. There was no reason for me not to believe her. No one in the family ever talked about Dad, so I never questioned what she told me. And whenever I tried to ask Mom about my father, she would start to cry. I didn't want to hurt her, so I kept most of my questions to myself.

Then, about six months ago, someone told me my father wasn't dead. So I confronted Mom. She said, "He wasn't ready to be a father." She said she had planned to tell me the truth someday, but she didn't want to "hurt" me.

I got so upset that I spent the rest of the night alone in my room. Mom came and knocked on my door, but I didn't want to talk to her.

I spent the next several days trying to get things straight in my own head. So many of the things I did were secretly for my father. I'd always wanted him to be proud of me—if he were alive. I guess I'd put together this fantasy picture of my dad.

But the person I had made up in my own mind didn't exist. It was like someone had died all over again. But, he was never dead. There was no perfect hero—just this man who'd taken off because he couldn't handle being my father. Why didn't he care? What did I ever do to him?

I kept thinking about Mom and what she could have done with her life if I'd never been born. Maybe my parents would have stayed together. I knew Mom still loved him. I wanted to die.

I began to plan how I would commit suicide.

Two days before I was going to kill myself, I wanted to make things up with Mom. I came home from school and told her I was sorry about getting so upset. She understood. She said she would have been upset if she were me. I told her I knew she'd given up a lot for me—and if I were dead she could live the rest of her life the way she wanted to. She asked if I'd thought about committing suicide, and I said, "Wouldn't that solve everyone's problems?"

Mom started crying. And then she grabbed me and asked me if I thought killing myself would change anything for me. She told me it would change *everything* for her. Her life would become a nightmare.

I learned a lot that night. I realized how much my morn loves me. She *wasn't* still in love with my father. And she didn't feel like she ever wanted to get married again. Mom told me that I keep her going, and she would rather have God take *her* life than to live without me. She said every day of my life I was helping her fulfill her dream of being a mother.

Then she reminded me of something she's said many times: "I will not always be right in how I try to teach you, but I always want to protect you from a lot of hurt."

Mom gave me a big hug. Both of us were sorry for everything that had happened. She told me my father really left because he was selfish—he didn't want to think about anyone other than himself. She didn't believe he really left because of me. He was just looking for an excuse, and if it wasn't me, in time he would have come up with another reason.

Things are going okay for me now that I know the truth. Mom and I are a lot closer. There are times when I really miss not having a father. I'll go over to a friend's house and his father will be there, and I can't help but wish I had a father.

But the man that left sixteen years ago was never a real father to me. Sometimes I wish I had a father to take his place. But it's okay.

David

In the Garden, One Flower

I had a dream last night
that I was standing in front of a wooden gate.
The gate was old and worn,
as if it had been used for many years,
and it appeared to open the way to a garden.
I couldn't make up my mind
if I wanted to go inside.
Then I heard someone say,
"Within this gate are flowers and trees,
alive with beauty greater

than anything you've ever seen."
Slowly I walked through the gate.
I couldn't believe my eyes!
I had never seen anything before
so perfect!
Except
my heart sank
when I looked down.
At my feet stood one flower,
plain and almost colorless,
large—too large—and wild grown,
out of place in this garden.
"How could this be? What went wrong?"
"This single flower will always grow in our garden,"
the voice said.
"It's the most precious of all the other flowers,
a reminder that nothing is perfect
but
God's love for you."

Dear David,

Your hurt required compassion and understanding toward your mom. I think she would agree that telling you the truth from the start would have avoided a lot of problems. But because of her love for you, she *thought* she was protecting you from your father's rejection.

It was a shock for you to find out the truth. But, in fact, you've been grieving for the "perfect" father that you had made up in your mind. And you didn't want to replace him with the father your mother told you about. The truth *does* hurt sometimes, but given a choice, I believe we'd all rather know the truth.

David, the problem was not you. It was with your father. I cannot answer for him, but he must have had some problems within himself that he couldn't handle. Maybe that's what made him react as if he didn't care. Nothing you did made him leave. You were only a small child. Your mother was most likely right when she told you he was just looking for an excuse. That doesn't make it right. But so often, people blame someone else for their feelings.

The conversation you had with your mother is a good example. More people should do what you did. When we face our problems and talk things out with a person we can trust and respect, we begin to find the answers we are searching for. We can also work out the conflicts we create in our minds. Sometimes we create worse problems for ourselves because we *think* we have an accurate picture—when really we *don't*. Just think, before you talked with your mom, you were going to end your life! Now you see things differently.

And I'd guess your mom sees some things differently, too. So often, single parents feel they have the full responsibility of loving and protecting their child. They want to make up for the parent who's missing. My own mother wanted everything to be so perfect for me, trying to "compensate" for my illness. Our moms and dads sometimes like to think they can wrap a shield around us to protect us from anything that hurts. But they can't. No one can protect us from hurts or disappointments.

Whenever I had to face a problem, I knew my mom was there. But really, it's the Lord who helps me make it through the hard times in my life. I think we forget how easy it is just to turn a problem over to God. How do you do this? By praying and asking the Lord to help you trust Him as He works things out according to His will.

I can understand how you feel as you watch your friends with their fathers. At fifteen, my heart ached. As I stood in front of my father, refusing to shed another tear, I said, "Daddy, just because you've left Mom doesn't mean you have to leave us kids." He never answered me. But he no longer remembered birthdays or Christmas presents or shared my dreams of going to college.

In the space of one afternoon, I no longer had a father. Nothing after that would have been as important to me as getting a hug and knowing that he loved me. I wished my father could have said just a few words that would have helped me understand. I wouldn't have felt so rejected and unworthy of being loved. I asked myself, *What's wrong with me that Daddy doesn't care?* At my friends' homes, I saw a mom and dad and kids—all together— just the way my family *should* have been. But I wasn't as upset about my parents getting a divorce as I was about not having a father, someone to go to when I had a problem.

Later, I discovered that my father didn't know how to tell us he was going through some personal problems. Although I tried to understand, it didn't make up for his absence. I know my family could have gotten through this much easier if we had continued to communicate more openly with one another.

Then one day I prayed, "Dear Father," instead of "Dear Jesus." At that very moment, I stopped praying. I hesitantly said those precious words again, "Dear Father." An empty gap filled in my heart, and I began to cry. For the first time in my life, I realized I *had* a father. A wonderful Father! In His faithfulness, He had always been there for me—protecting me, loving me, and healing my wounds.

So often we search for answers in empty places when our heavenly Father can help us understand situations we cannot change. It was the love of my true Father that taught me *I am someone,* and *I am worthy of being loved.* He also changed my hurting heart to a forgiving heart.

David, you also have a Father. Those of us who have longed for a parent can know we have a perfect heavenly Father who is watching us grow, a Father who will continue to be at our side while He molds us to carry out His plan for our lives.

There are so many things my heavenly Father has taught me—but the most important lesson I've learned was remembering that He is *my Father* and I am *His child.*

> Did I tell you about a man named Jesus?
> He fed multitudes.
> The winds and the water obeyed Him.
> He was strong, yet humble.
> In His wisdom, He knew how to answer every man. In
> His heart,
>> there is a place
>> for every one of His children—
>> where burdens are lighter
>> and every joy is greater. We are the children
>> He holds in the palm of His hand.

Chapter 15

A Hiding Place

"Grandpa, how long has this window been open in the old barn?"

"Oh, for a long time. I took down part of the wood I nailed up just in case anyone decided to use it for a hiding place."

"What do you mean, a hiding place?"

"You were too little to remember, but once when your older brother was growing up, he was looking for a hiding place. One night he wanted to get out of doing his chores so he could leave early for a basketball game at school. He'd already put his chores off for several days, so your mom wasn't going to let him go until he'd done his work. Well, he got mad and felt no one cared about what *he* wanted to do. He made up his mind he'd hide out in the old barn until morning came so he could run away. When everyone thought he was out doing his chores, he took off for the barn. He noticed a storm was coming up, so he slammed the barn door tight.

"Inside, it was completely dark, and he couldn't see anything at all. He tried to get out, but the old, rusty latch had locked from the outside. About that time, he was getting scared. He could hear the lightning and thunder outside. Being stuck in the old barn wasn't part of his plan. He yelled for the family, but there was not any way we could have heard him. When your mom couldn't find your brother, she thought he had gone to the game without telling her. Meanwhile, your brother was cold and scared, but he found his way to a corner in the barn where he had a chance to think about what he'd done.

"He began to realize that if he had done his chores, none of this would have happened. And he could have gone to the game with his friends. He wasn't sure when he would get out of that old barn. And he didn't treasure the idea of spending the night there with a storm coming up. He began to remember the fun times he used to have with his family, and he even remembered the times your mom asked him what he wanted to do. He realized that his mom *did* care about him. He was feeling bad about running away, because he would have been leaving everyone who cared about him. He was so tired he fell asleep.

"When it got late, your mom was worried. After calling his friends, she called me. The storm hadn't let up, but she insisted we go out and look for him. After the unsuccessful search, we sat up all night, and I watched her walk the floor. I knew if something happened to your brother, she'd blame herself.

"At first light, the storm had passed. She grabbed her coat and began to walk across the farm. I thought I'd better follow her in case she needed me. About that time, your brother woke up. He tried again to get out, but he couldn't. He began to yell for your mom. I couldn't hear him, but she could. I watched her run toward the barn as fast as she could. Once she opened the door, he flew into her arms. By the time I got there, I wanted to tan his hide—but your mom wouldn't hear of it.

"That night I overheard your mom and brother when they said good night. 'I'm really sorry, Mom,' your brother said. Your mother responded, 'I was so afraid because I thought I'd lost you!'"

Maybe

Maybe we ought to hug others
a little more often
and tell them, "I love you."

Chapter 16

A Reason to Live

My arms held her as she repeated the words over and over again, "I'm so tired of hurting." As I wiped the tears from her face, I gently spoke these words: "Do you know there isn't a tear that falls that God doesn't hear or see?" I saw her eyes look to me as if her heart was asking if these words were really true.

Her bedroom door opened a crack. I watched her fouryear-old brother open the door just wide enough to come in. With all the concern in the world on his little face, he stood hesitantly by the door. I stretched out my arms, giving him permission to come closer. As I hugged him, both he and his sister turned their eyes toward mine. I smiled and asked, "Would you like me to tell you a story?" In the pause that followed, I saw the light shining through the bedroom window and remembered Christ's words: "I am the light of the world" (John 8:12).

Silently I prayed, *Father, fill my heart with your words.*

Their young faces watched my every move, waiting for me to begin. And this is the story I told:

"Once upon a time, there was a boy and girl who lived in two different parts of the world. They were thoughtful and kind to everyone they met. Though they had a lot of friends, neither one could see himself as others did. They were always giving their love away, but never thought of the love that others had for them. In their minds, they were never good enough or attractive enough, and they felt their dreams would never come true. When they were happy, they brightened everyone's days; but they also had times when they would cry when no one was around.

"Even though they lived very far apart and had never met each other, they began to share the same feelings. They decided they didn't want to live anymore, so they chose to take their own lives in their hands and commit suicide.

"That afternoon, the girl's mother had gone shopping after work and saw a lovely sweater she thought would look beautiful on her daughter. She drove home, looking forward to surprising her daughter with a gift. As she walked into her daughter's room, she pressed the sweater tightly against her heart. There was silence for a moment as she absorbed the painful truth of what she was seeing. Then a long pause separated each word as the mother cried, "I . . . love . . . you . . . and . . . I . . . bought . . . this . . . sweater . . . for . . . you!" She laid the sweater across her daughter and rocked her cold, dead body in her arms.

"Meanwhile, the boy's little brother had run through the front door, calling out his older brother's name. As the little boy walked down the hall, he saw that his brother's bedroom door was open, so he went in to say hello. There on the floor, in a pool of blood, lay his brother's body. Trembling in shock, the little boy turned and ran out of the house into the rain.

"Only moments passed before his parents came home. The rain and the tears now covered their small son's face. He spoke, and the parents ran to their older son. As the father lifted his older son in his arms, the little boy cried, 'We can't play anymore.'

"Now together, the boy and girl stood at an open gate, searching for a voice they could not find. They turned around—then around again. But the voice continued echoing, 'If they could see our faces, feel our pain that will never heal . . .' No other words were spoken as their feelings of uncertainty grew stronger.

"Finally, the silence was broken. 'What should we do?' asked the girl. Before the boy could answer her, they were silenced by another voice. 'It was not God's time for you to be with Him. You chose the time. Look back on what your actions have done and all that you've missed. Both of you had lost your trust in God for your future. You also forgot to pray. Even though God already knows our hurts and disappointments, you still needed to tell Him in prayer; that is the beginning of your willingness to receive God's direction and not your own. It was God's desire for you both to fulfill His will for your lives, to discover that He wanted to be with you always. If you had only looked beyond the pain and trusted in Him, He could have shown you how much there was to live for. The love He has for us would have carried you through this time in your lives. Jesus did not come just to be our Savior, but He also came to be in our lives.'"

With the story told and with a heart that was filled with the reminder of God's unfailing love for us, I asked the girl in my arms, "Do you know how precious you are to God?" With tears of hope she cried, "Now I know I have a reason to live."

> Daniel was a white and graceful seagull.
> He had everything to live for.
> But things didn't go right.
> He gave up.
> He didn't want to live anymore.
> The other seagulls thought,
> "If Daniel gave up, we should give up, too."
> One seagull thought for a very long time, though.
> While the others folded up their wings
> miserably,
> he kept his eyes open wide and his wings free to fly.
> And he was the only one who felt
> when the new wind of morning
> brought freshness and
> lift.

Chapter 17

THE COLORS OF
YOUR HEART

As I walked past the chapel today, I stopped to look at the light as it bounced colors off the stained glass window. The colors were beautiful as they fell so gently. I ran to look at all the other windows, but only one reflected the light. Then I thought, "The colors must be inside."

A silent prayer ran through my head: *Please, Lord. Have the door open so I can get in.*

My excitement grew as I reached for the knob—and the door quietly opened. The moment I stepped inside, my excitement slowed and changed into reverence. Colors graced the aisle that led me to the altar. At the foot of the altar lay a color, shaped like a heart. I was aware of His holy presence. Raising my eyes toward the cross, I knelt.

"Lord, what are the colors of my heart? How broken has my path been to your altar? If my heart loses its radiance, show me *your* light. Always lead me on the path that comes to your altar." I lifted my hands to wipe my tears, for I'd felt His love despite my unworthiness. I stood and walked down the aisle, realizing my love for the Lord would reflect the colors of my heart. If I trust in Him, He *will* direct all the paths of my life.

When I reached the door, I turned to look at the altar one last time. It reminded me about the altar inside each one of us, the silent space where God meets us—where He accepts us and the prayer we offer to Him.

Then I swung the door open wide and ran down the steps. My heart was filled with joy! I was taking the Lord with me.

> I hurt in the depth of my soul
> Where no one can reach me.
> I cry and no one sees my pain.
> I long to be held as a mother holds her sweet child.
> I comfort others but no one comforts me.
> There is no tender touch
> No loving embrace;
> I pray, but the answer doesn't come.
> In the beating of my heart that gives me life, I long to
> crawl out of this pit and live again;
> I want to be saved.
> Look at me and hear my heart

Chapter 18

FROM THE DIARY OF AMANDA MICHAELS

y name is Amanda Michaels, and I've always believed there were two of me—two different people living inside of me. I've always known this, and I've always felt as though it was *us* against the world. She holds my secrets I can't remember and memories I don't want to recall. There were times I needed her, but she couldn't help me.

Perhaps I wanted to die; I wanted both of us to die. I have moments of visions from my life that appear before me in a flash and are gone just as fast. It seems that she takes them away and makes me forget so I don't have to remember—but I still do. The truth is I am living because this other person living inside of me does exist.

I don't remember why it happened. To this day, I still don't have an answer. Perhaps the answer is simply because he could. All the times before, there was never a good reason, so why would this time be any different? I was beaten as often as other children were hugged. His verbal abuse came every time he looked at me. Did I remind him of something evil, or was it only the inner Satan inside of him that saw me? He said I would never amount to anything. After all, who was I? I was the daughter he created in my mother's belly, and this gave him the right to imprison me with his insanity. I wasn't allowed to openly think or question his actions. He was God in our house, and who would question God? He was the preacher, loved by his congregation and feared by his children who trembled at his every glance. I was alone. The truth was never spoken in our home, and if I did tell someone, who would believe me? We lived the truth in our house, but we were not allowed to share our secrets with the outside world. We lived as if the pain in our home didn't exist.

Our family never stayed anywhere very long. If my father wasn't happy, that gave him enough reason to pick up in the middle of the night and leave. I changed schools at least once a year, sometimes twice. When he left one church, it was never very long before he would find another one. He was handsome and knew how to act as if God Himself approved of him. I was only fourteen, and on this day, I remember the sun shining so brightly. I felt it cover me as I walked home from school. What is it about sunshine and its warm light that fills you up with goodness? It was a gift, just for me, just for that moment. Perhaps I was given this small gift because what happened next delivered me to the gates of hell.

I walked into the house and heard the quiet sound you hear when no one else is there. The silence of being alone was something I cherished. I felt safe. It was my hiding place, and I didn't care why or when the others would come back. I knew I wouldn't be alone long. I went into the bathroom to take a shower.

I was a size six, with a fully developed body. I never saw myself as pretty. How could I? I wasn't real, only pretend real. I don't remember a day my father didn't tell me I wasn't pretty. The control he had over my thoughts was absolute. I never allowed myself to think anything different than the evil he told me. I stood in the shower, letting the water run over me.

I never heard the bathroom door open. As fast as you can be surprised and unprepared for the strike of lighting, the shower door opened, and I heard the popping sound he would make with the cut leather belt he used to punish us. I knew what would happen next. Satan was there.

As quickly as I turned to him, he struck me, and my body slammed against the wet tile. My head hit the wall, and I faced the corner of the shower with my hands stretched out, holding me in place. I dared not to move out of fear of what he would do next. Over and over again, he hit me with the strips of leather at the ends of the belt. I wasn't going to let him see me cry. Even though I couldn't stop my tears, I wasn't going to allow him to see my face.

One never knows how long eternity really is, but for me, I couldn't hold myself up any longer, and my bloody body began to slide down the wet wall. He had beaten me until the blood started to run across my feet, and as I moved down the shower, he hit me across my back. Then he stopped. I don't know if it was the hand of God that intervened or if beating me simply did not amuse him anymore.

My head filled with short sounds of me trying to catch my breath. In and out, in and out, I fought for air and my whole body shook. The bottom of the shower was filled with blood.

I was afraid to move, and I would never turn and look at him. He could kill me before I'd turn around and look at him. There was silence, and then he left.

I don't know what made him stop, but I was afraid if I stayed there he would come back. Somehow I managed to get up and cover myself as I went back to my room. I could hear voices, but no one saw me. I went to my room and secured the door. I lay there, and in my tears, and through the brokenness of my soul, I cried out in silence. I couldn't let anyone hear me. I couldn't say a word.

I never left my room that night, and no one came to me. I wonder what lie he told about me. It didn't matter because I wanted to be alone. I wanted him to leave me alone. I didn't belong with him. I wasn't like him. Something wasn't right. I couldn't be his daughter. He wasn't my father; he never acted like a father, not to me anyway.

I lay across my bed, covered by my blankets and held by the part of me that carried me through the pain. I didn't care if the morning never came, but it did. Somehow, against my wishes, I lived through the night. As if it was second nature, without thoughts of the shame, I put on enough clothing to cover the marks the belts made across my body. I walked out of my room as if it never happened. After all these years, I knew how to play the game, and I played the game well.

It was Sunday morning. Now that I was older, I could help in the church nursery. I would do anything that kept me from being in the sanctuary, listening to my father preach. I couldn't help looking at him and asking myself how he could say those words in front of God and the congregation and be a completely different person behind the closed doors of our home.

The nursery was a safe place. One doesn't usually think of a nursery as a place that would change your life, but for me, that is exactly what happened. I'll never forget the day I first met Tommy. He was three, and he was born with a rare deformity. I don't know if he was mentally challenged. No one ever told me. His body was twisted beyond anything I had ever seen. His motor skills could be compared to a six-month-old baby. When I first saw Tommy, he frightened me. The bones in his legs and arms were twisted, and his legs wrapped around each other. His face was distorted, but it was his eyes that drew me to him. His eyes saw me, and I saw him. After seeing Tommy for the first time, I couldn't get him off my mind. That little boy was helpless. He was like me.

No one really saw him, not in the real sense of the word. They saw what he looked like, but I don't think they saw his heart. We had more in common than he knew. Tommy couldn't speak and neither could I.

The next Sunday, Tommy's mother brought him back to church. I was hoping I would see him again. This time when I looked at Tommy, his eyes reached out to me. I tenderly touched him. I was no longer afraid of what I saw because I looked upon a little boy who was more precious than all of the other babies in the nursery.

We all have the power to love immediately. For me, looking into his eyes, I fell in love. Without asking, I picked him up and held him in my arms. I remember Mama was in the nursery with me. She was surprised by my actions, but I think when she saw us, she couldn't help but let me hold him. He wasn't very big. I rocked him and sang to him. His eyes just watched me, and in that moment, there was a special bond between us, an unconditional love for each other. Somehow I felt he saw me like no one else did.

I remember, at the end of the church service, his mother walked in and was surprised to see Tommy in my arms. Her silence made me feel like I may have done something wrong. I told her I thought Tommy wanted to be held. I don't think she was upset with me. I think someone else holding her child was a strange sight.

It was a couple of days later when Tommy's mother wanted me to babysit for her. I was a little surprised by her invitation but was glad to be able to see him again. When I arrived, Tommy was in his bed. After his mom left, I picked him up and held him in my arms. He had been a little squirmy, but when he settled down, all his attention was on me. There was a country song playing in the background, so we began to two-step. I held him, and we slowly danced around the room. I'd take two steps out and two steps back.

When we stopped dancing, I made up stories about a little boy who was a dragon slayer. He wasn't like all the other boys because God made him different because he had a special job to do. I told Tommy I didn't know what his special job might be, but both of us would know one day. He looked at me as if he understood everything I was saying. It hadn't been more than a couple of hours before Tommy's mother returned and found him fast asleep in my arms. I just wanted to hold him for as long as I could.

The next day, Mom brought me the news that Tommy had died in the night. I couldn't believe her words. Tommy was dead. He was in my arms the night before. We danced together. He was so peaceful and happy and perfect. His mom said his heart gave out.

It would be the last time we would be together. I loved him, and he was gone. I was alone again.

I promised myself, he would always be with me. The next few days, all I could think about was Tommy and what he gave me. Tommy taught me about the power of hope. He showed me, even when I thought things were bad, I had so much to be thankful for. I could make my life better just by being me. I would never forget the way I loved him, and I believe he loved me back. Perhaps he knew much more than I did about living. I wish he could have stayed longer, but for Tommy, God's timing was better than mine. What the world saw in Tommy may not have been pretty, but God saw Tommy's heart. He was a little boy who simply loved. I'm always reminded of Tommy's strength when I need to be strong myself.

When the cloud of my grief began to lift, I found out my family was running away again. The last several weeks around my home had been calm. It had been a little over a month since he had beaten me so badly, and I had time to myself to tuck the pain of losing Tommy away in my heart.

The old saying, "There is always a calm before the storm," was lived out in my home. My father was due to return from a trip any day now, and I had a strange feeling something big was coming home with him. I don't think even I was prepared for his announcement. We were moving. This time it wasn't because he wasn't happy. I think he was just restless. We had been in the same place for almost a year and a half. The people in the church really liked him. We had a nice parsonage, and for the first time, Mama seemed happy.

His announcement seemed so far beyond anything I would have ever imagined. We were moving to Detroit. I knew better than to question him. Once he made up his mind, that was it; there was no going back. We had lived in many difference places, but we always seemed to find ourselves around the coast of North Carolina.

Detroit was bigger than life. I couldn't imagine living there. This was the South; that was the North. We didn't talk like them, and it was freezing. Did it matter to anyone else that I didn't want to go? He could go. They could all go. I would be more than happy to just stay put. I would do something, anything, and live anywhere if I didn't have to go. I was going to have to go to high school in Detroit. This news was major, and I was certain he had not thought of what a difference it would be for my sisters and me. Why would he? He never thought of others before. He had all the right answers, and I was to do what he said, nothing more. He had arranged everything, and we were moving.

Mama didn't say very much that day. I saw her look around her nice home, and somehow, I think she knew things would never be the same, but she never said so. She never said anything against him. If she did, I never heard her. He beat us kids, but I never saw him beat her. Even so, behind closed doors, I heard words so hateful he might as well have struck her. She told me once she wanted to leave, but with no place to go and no money to live on, she had no other choice but to stay.

In a moment of courage, if she had a safe place, she would have taken her children and run for all of our lives. When I look back on it now, I know Mama was just as broken as we were.

I'm sure it's no surprise when I say I thought about dying every month and sometimes every day, but that was before Tommy. Because Tommy saw something in me I didn't see in myself, he gave me purpose to go on. The memory of Tommy will be my lifeline for the rest of my life. I'd come to realize we all must choose to live, or even just exist, because everyone deals with pain and disappointment. Now I knew the pain goes away and doesn't last forever. I learned not to believe the lies I may tell myself because I do have worth. I'm reminded of Tommy who taught me every life has value. Everyone has to deal with disappointment and pain. The important lesson in all of this is to know pain does go away and life does get better. It's important to hold on and believe in a future you can't see at the moment.

I think sometimes we just need to dance and keep dancing. Step out in hope and dance the two-step all night long if you need to. Be your own cheerleader, and stop believing the lies you tell yourself. You are in control of the conversation in your head. Tell yourself you have worth and you can make a brighter future for yourself. Even at our lowest points in life, there is someone who can walk with us through our pain. His name is Jesus. Pray and be honest before the Lord, and let Him know how you really feel.

If Tommy could talk, he would tell you how much your life is worth, and when you've been given the gift of life, God has a plan for you. If we take our life before we grow up, we miss the blessings God has planned for us. We need to believe in this gift and know it's true—even if we feel we have no reason to live.

I have memorized a great verse that helps me to remember this truth: "'For I know the plans I have for you,' declares the Lord, 'plans to prosper you and not to harm you, plans to give you hope and a future'" (Jer. 29:11). I have this verse posted all over my room and on my bathroom mirror. God has a plan for you, greater than you can imagine. Hold on because the pain will go away, and you will have a destiny greater than you could ever imagine. Give God a chance to direct your life. Hold on because your faith ride will be awesome.

I'm so ready to find out what God has planned for me, but in the meantime, I'm going to continue to live and believe in who I will be. Where will God take me if I allow Him in my life? When negative thoughts come into my mind, I simply take a two-step out in hope, as if moving away from something that could hurt me, away from thoughts that could bring me down or make me lose hope.

Perhaps Tommy's purpose was to teach me to always remember I can dance when Tommy couldn't. I plan on following his lead and being the best me I can be. When I get hurt, I tell myself not to give up hope because there is power in hope, and no matter what I may go through, there is a plan God has laid out for my life that only I can fulfill. This same truth is real in your life.

I'm dreaming of a future I've never imagined before, and it makes my hurt seem smaller. I will not give up. There was hope in Tommy's eyes, even though he dealt with hurt every day of his life. I saw a light inside of him that was beautiful and worth living for. Tommy will never know he saved my life, but I hope our story will save yours. Give yourself a chance, and take pride in how far you've come. Have faith in how far God will take you. Step away from your pain and two-step for a little while. Keep dancing, and hope will feel closer. Your pain will not be so bad.

My journal entry on the day Tommy died:

Tommy,
I'll never forget what you gave me.
You taught me how special life truly is.
I know one day I'll see you again. Rest in peace,
Sweet little boy.
Amanda

Chapter 19

A Letter
Just for You

Our walk is over, but I will always have a special place in my heart for you. We've been through a lot together—you and I—tears and laughter, sorrow and hope. If I could only go around the world and share precious moments with each and every one of you! I can't, of course, but God can.

Depression was once explained to me as if a large concert block was sitting on your chest and you couldn't get up.

You tell yourself you can't get up. The truth is, you can, but you listen to the lie inside your mind and refuse to lift the block off your chest because it's easier to let it sit there and hold you down. This way, you don't have to face seeing people or talking to them or explaining for the hundredth time you really don't care about anything at all to someone who cares too much and doesn't seem to understand why you just can't snap out of it.

You are afraid to go out into the world and get hurt again. You feel safer hiding in your own little world and not being a part of other lives, so you just drift through. Fear takes over any hope you have left.

Think about this, everything you want is on the other side of fear. Once you move through your own fear, your life begins to get better and you are taking part in your life instead of just letting one day lead to another and another. Make a new plan for your life and begin to imagine yourself being an active part of that new life you have planned. Make a list of all the things you would like to do, even if they seem impossible. List all of your dreams, big or small. Nothing can stop you. Keep dreaming and make your list as long as you like. Now add goals you would like to achieve at some point in your life. When you are finished, put your list somewhere you can see it and be reminded of your dreams and goals. You don't want to miss out on all that God has planned for you. Your list is your hope for tomorrow. You wouldn't want to miss out on any of these events coming true in your life. God will help you get there if you ask Him.

No one lives a life free of disappointment or pain. Everyone struggles with something at different times.

I want you to remember: No matter how unworthy you may feel, or how often you think you've failed to measure up, hold the truths of Christ close to your heart.

You are special to God. Because of His love for us, He sent His only Son so that we would have eternal life through Christ. He created you in His image, and you are the only one that can carry out His plans for your life.

What does God want from us? He wants us to love Him. When you can't find a reason to go on, *just love Him.* When you feel you've disappointed God and everyone around, *just love Him.*

When you feel overwhelmed, ask for help. Asking for help is a sign of strength, not weakness. Asking for help to get through your struggles will make you feel stronger, and the pain you feel will not last as long. As you trust in God, He'll give you a reason to live. When you think you've failed, you'll find His forgiveness. And when you think you can't go on, you'll find His strength. There is no burden God cannot carry, no pain He cannot bear. If you are dealing with thoughts of taking your own life, there are suicide hotlines you can call, day or night. (You can find their number on the Internet and your call will be confidential.) Find someone at church to confide in or turn to a friend you can be honest with. You don't need to feel ashamed. You are not alone; everyone deals with pain and disappointment at some point in his life. How we handle these times in our lives makes all the difference on how we get through them.

God created you in your mother's womb. He loves you more than you could ever imagine. He has a plan for your life, and if you will only reach out to Him, you will find that your life counts and you have so many reasons to live. Replace the voices in your head with a positive message; tell yourself you have purpose and God has a plan for you and you are going to see it through.

Trust me, I have lived through the pain, and I know you may not see the plan right now. I'm asking you to give yourself some time. Tell yourself you have a destiny in front of you and you are going to wait and find out what it is. Ask God to put His desires in your heat, and I promise you He will. Your life counts, so don't miss out on the plan God has for you.

Now, go out and live. Your life can be full and exciting. Replace the lies in your head with the truth of God's love. You are the child of a King who has always loved you and always will.

There's a special letter I've been saving till now to share with you. I met the young woman who wrote it in Chicago when I'd gone there to speak at a teen retreat. She was seventeen, so alive and beautiful. Raised in a Christian home, she'd attended a Christian high school. Until the weekend of the retreat, she was unable to share her problems with anyone. Now she realized that reaching out when she needed help was the first step to finding the answers she desperately needed.

I shared her tears—and how well I knew her pain! We took a long walk together, and that night the Lord helped her share some of her deepest hurts and disappointments. And in God's way, as we talked and prayed, He opened up her thoughts and met her questions with answers of possibilities. I want to share with you a small part of her letter that is so special for me:

> About life at home—you were right! Things are so much better. We still have our bad days, but they're fewer and further between. And they're made easier because I know my heavenly Father is looking down on me, longing to hold me in His arms and make everything right.
>
> One night, when I was crying, I thought about how much it must have hurt God when He created me to know that I'd have to hurt this much. He wouldn't have let it happen to me if there wasn't a purpose. So I think He must have something wonderful planned for me to do. I only wish the process weren't so painful!

"The Lord will fulfill his purpose for me; your love, O
Lord, endures forever—do not abandon the works of your
hands" *(Ps. 138:8, NIV)*.

She had chosen the words of David. In David's greatest
time of need, he praised the Lord and cried out to Him in faith,
knowing that God would not abandon him and that He would
carry out His purpose for David's life. She'd learned that loving
God doesn't give us a life without hurts or disappointments.
But God can help us make it through those times, and things
do get better.

When we look to God for His answers, we have a reason to
live as we wait for His purpose to be revealed in our lives. In
every burden I've ever known, I have found a blessing and a
purpose. It wasn't always at the time I thought it would be—
but it always came when I was ready to receive it.

Never give up! When God takes something away, He gives
us something else in return. Live with the confidence that God
holds all your tomorrows. Fill your mind with His purpose for
your life and then you'll know His reason to live.

Keep your eyes open wide, your hands free to help a friend,
and your heart filled with all the good things God intended for
you. And always, *always believe in yourself and in your dreams.*

"Be joyful in hope, patient in affliction, faithful in prayer"
(Rom. 12:12, NIV).

Has the Lord carried you through a difficult time? Has this
book touched your heart? I anxiously look forward to hearing
from you.

If you are interested in having me come to your church or organization, please contact me.

Only you can fulfill God's plan for your life. He has given you everything you need to carry out His plan. Do not miss out on God's best for you. His best for you will be your greatest joy and peace.

God Bless You Today,
Donalyn Powell
www.donalynpowell.com
donalynpowell@aol.com

> He shall be as the light of the morning;
> A cloudless sunrise
> When the tender grass
> Springs forth upon the earth;
> As sunshine after rain.
> And it is my family
> He has chosen!
> Yes, God has made
> An everlasting covenant with me;
> His agreement is eternal, final, sealed.
> He will constantly look after
> My safety and success.
> *2 Samuel 23:4–5, TLB*

Chapter 20

A FINAL WORD: THE FACTS ABOUT SUICIDE

5:30 *a.m.* The Emergency Room was as noisy as ever. A patient was rushed in on a rescue squad stretcher, with the crew pumping on his chest and bagging oxygen into his lungs. I hurried into the cardiac room behind the ER doctor and noted the patient with surprise and anguish. He could not have been more then sixteen or seventeen years old!

Numbly pitching in with vigorous effort (though we already knew our efforts to be futile), I noticed all of the doctors, nurses, and technicians avoided the pain in each other's eyes. The rope burns on his neck told the story: he had hung himself.

Still I kept feeling for a pulse that would not come. I wanted desperately to make him live, to bring him back to life. *To give anew the gift of life—that's what we are here for,* I kept thinking. But we could not reverse the lack of oxygen to his brain. We could not give him thoughts or hopes or dreams again. He had extinguished them all, by his own hand, in a moment of pain—with a piece of rope.

I looked at the family, huddling together hopelessly, and I will never forget their shocked faces, the depth of their pain. Nor will I forget the police, standing awkwardly in the background, who had to question the parents because of his violent death.

Suicide now ranks as the second leading cause of death among fifteen- to nineteen-year-olds in the United States, representing a 41 percent increase over the last decade.[1] Even these startling statistics are probably far below the actual number, because suicides and suicidal attempts are vastly under-reported.

Between 50 to 75 percent of the adolescents who attempt suicide suffer from depression. Teens with conduct disorders are the second largest group of those who commit or attempt suicide, and those suffering from psychotic disorders, such as schizophrenia, represent the third largest group.[2] Teens considered at higher risk for suicide include those involved in substance abuse, those who have suffered physical abuse or molestation, those who have a history of chronic depression, teens with generally poor communication skills, and teens with chronic illnesses. One retrospective study revealed that young women who had babies before the age of seventeen had ten times the average number of suicide attempts.[3] Another study

1   "Teen Suicide Increases: Risk and Causes Identified," *American Family Physician* 36, No. 1 (July 1987): 272.
2   Sari Staver, "Help Prevent Teen Suicides, MDs Urged," *American Medical News* 23/30 (November 1984): 39–40.
3   Iris F. Litt, "Suicide in Adolescents," *Resident and Staff Physician*, July 1985, 1pc.

indicated that one in twelve inner-city adolescents interviewed had tried to commit suicide.[4]

Classic symptoms of depression in teenagers may include changes in eating and sleeping habits, withdrawal from friends and family, and poor concentration—often manifested by a drop in school performance. Radical changes in personality and psychosomatic complaints are other frequent symptoms.[5] Older teenagers often show these symptoms; however, they may additionally show irritability, lethargy, and decreased concern with their surroundings, relationships, or personal hygiene.[6]

Unfortunately, not all teens demonstrate the classic warning signs of depression. Sudden rebellious behavior, truancy, multiple physical complaints, "daredevil" stunts, sexual promiscuity, frequent accidents, or a sudden frenzy of activity may all be alternative symptoms for teenage depression.[7] Signals of such depression may not be noticed unless careful attention is given to adolescent behavior changes, including seemingly blatant ones, like writing about death or giving away prized possessions.

The following is just one scenario but is typical of a teenager's final plea for help:

> No one really noticed the gradual changes in Richard, a high school student from a large, well-respected family. All of the children were bright, and Richard was one of the brightest.

---

4   "Teen Suicide Increases," 272.
5   Staver, 40.
6   H. Norman Wright, "The Crisis of Suicide," in *Crisis Counseling* (San Bernardino: Here's Life Publishers, 1985), 106–107.
7   American Academy of Pediatrics, Committee on Adolescence, Michael T. Cohen, Chairperson, "Teenage Suicide," *Pediatrics* 66 (July 1980): 144.

His obvious intelligence contrasted sharply with the sudden decline in his grades during his senior year. Fellow students were puzzled and concerned about laziness when his grades went from straight As to Cs and Ds. The teachers wondered why such a nice boy had suddenly chosen such a gruesome essay topic as death.

Often a student who did not fit in with others, Richard was always gentle about the sometimes cruel teasing he received from classmates. Yet he withdrew noticeably from those few he called friends. His appearance degenerated till he looked disheveled and sloppy. People thought he either slept in his clothes—or he never slept.

Near the end of the year, Richard suddenly seemed to develop overwhelming energy. In a frenzy of activity, he changed from taking piano lessons to trying to put together a band. When he and his classmates began receiving college acceptances, he showed none of the enthusiasm of the other students, although he was accepted into a top school.

When Richard died shortly thereafter, from an "accident with a gun," surely the real accident was that no one who knew him realized the hundred subtle ways he had asked for their help.

There are no really definitive reasons "why" a teenager takes his or her own life. Often, a suicide appears to be an attempt to resolve a conflict by which the teen feels entrapped. This conflict may involve friends, parents, boyfriends or girlfriends, or even school and church groups. Personal losses, such as the death of a loved one, disruption of the family unit by divorce, or any matter that the teen perceives to be a personal, irrevocable failure, may become a precipitating event. Guilt or fear of the consequences of such matters as legal involvements or pregnancy may, again, create an overwhelming conflict in an adolescent's life.[8]

Other factors that currently contribute to the escalating suicide rate must surely include media glamorization of violence and death. Teenagers may romanticize the attention or help they will receive from suicide without realizing the finality of such an act.[9]

Many people consider suicide, at least fleeting thoughts of it, at some painful point of their lives. Teens may commit suicide in an effort to stop emotional pain, unable to see through the moment to know they *can* survive the pain without ending their lives.

Although five to eight times as many females as males attempt suicide, four times as many males actually commit suicide. These statistics probably reflect the more lethal methods males choose, including firearms and hanging, as compared to medication overdoses, which are the most common method attempted by females.[10] Many actual suicide attempts by adolescents are fraught with mixed feelings, a struggle between a wish to die and a hope of rescue. Therefore, they can give off incongruent signals: while they may try to take their lives by highly lethal means, they may also offer many advance warning signals in the hope of being discovered and rescued in time.[11]

The key to prevention of teen suicides is to alert and mobilize parents, teachers, friends, health personnel, and other

---

8   Robert B. Shearin, "Suicide and Depression," in *Handbook of Adolescent Medicine* (Kalamazoo: Upjohn Co., 1983), 131.

9   American Academy of Pediatrics, "Teenage Suicide," 144.

10   Ibid., 144.

11   Leon Eisenberg, "Adolescent Suicide: On Taking Arms Against a Sea of Troubles," *Pediatrics* 66 (July 1980): 319.

potential rescuers, teaching them to recognize high-risk teens or behavioral clues preceding a suicide attempt and how to intervene.[12] Surprisingly, an estimated 80 percent of suicide victims mention their intent before their attempts.[13]

Of course, any non-suicidal adolescent may have some of the same behavior characteristics as one contemplating suicide. Therefore, we must ask in order to know. Remember that thoughts of suicide need to be brought into the open for you to be able to help. Asking about suicide will not plant the idea of suicide in the mind of someone who is not already contemplating it. It will often offer the relief of being able to talk about it to someone who *is* thinking about it. Take a supportive attitude and encourage a young person; that's the best first step. Remember that people contemplating suicide are usually ambivalent about living or dying.[14] Therefore, they need suggestions of hope and the support of someone who will point out reasons to live.

If you suspect an adolescent is suicidal, maintain frequent and open contact. Encourage him to call or to stop by in person. Listen to everything he has to say—and then offer hope. For example, "I'm glad we can talk about this," and "I believe there is help for you." Try to pinpoint the problems and listen to the story, his or her previous attempts to cope, and what the current problem is. Try to focus on his or her feelings and try not to moralize. Exploring his reasons for wanting to die can help to break up feelings of overwhelming helplessness into more manageable portions.[15]

---

12 Staver, 39.
13 Wright, 100.
14 Eisenberg, 319.
15 Wright, 108–110.

Referral to professionals trained in intervention is a wise course of action. Professional intervention will include assessment of the teenager's risk of suicide, treatment, help through counseling, and possibly medication. A teen may be treated as an outpatient or recommended for hospitalization, according to the assessed danger. Important aspects of any treatment include mobilizing family support for therapy, discussion, and increasing observation of the patient.[16] The patient's home must be cleared of any potentially lethal weapons.[17] The counselor may ask the patient and family to initiate a "contract" to assure the patient's safety during the time of healing. Friends who offer acceptance and support are also of major importance.

Some mistaken ideas about suicide include:

1. *"People who talk about suicide don't do it."* Remember—80 percent of those who commit suicide have communicated their intent previously.
2. *"Suicide is only a danger in certain classes or ages."* No—suicide crosses all ages and classes.[18]
3. *"Improvement after depression means the risk has passed."* Fifty percent of suicides occur within three months of the first crisis.
4. *"Christians don't commit suicide."* Christians are still human—subject to emotional pain and problems in life.[19]

What else can be done? The number of susceptible teens is now higher than ever before, due to rampant alcohol and

---

16   Shearin, 130–131.
17   Eisenberg, 317.
18   Jerry Johnston, *Why Suicide?* (Nashville: Oliver-Nelson Books, 1987), 135–137.
19   Wright, 100–101.

drug abuse, broken homes, and the glamorization of violence on television and in movies—in addition to the usual pressures of adolescence, including sexual activity and peer pressure. For society to restore the "taboo" against suicide rather than to contribute to these factors would help, as would removal of easy access to lethal weapons.[20]

One unique problem with teen suicides is their tendency to "cluster." After one teenage suicide, multiple suicides tend to follow in the same area in rapid sequence. If the first teen was popular, his or her death tends to be romanticized by teens and may spur a rash of similar deaths. For example, in 1983 eight teenagers took their lives in a Dallas suburb within three months;[21] in another Texas city in early 1984, six teens took their lives. Across the continent, ten New York teens in Westchester took their lives over an eight-month period.[22] We must, therefore, emphasize to teens the hope of living and minimize the associated sensationalism of death by suicide.

The epidemic of teenage suicides in the United States destroys not only the lives and future potential of approximately 5,400 teenagers each year, but it tragically ravages the lives of their friends and families after their deaths.[23] I was reminded of this fact while talking with a beautiful high school student who had been very close to her brother. In the two years following his death by suicide, she had managed to struggle through her own numbness and her friends' awkwardness to achieve high grades and a college scholarship and to get elected to an office

---

20   Eisenberg, 319.
21   Michael Doan, "As 'Cluster Suicides' Take Toll of Teenagers," in collaboration with Sarah Peterson, *U.S. News & World Report*, 12 November 1984, 499–550.
22   Staver, 39.
23   "National Center for Health Statistics: Advance Report of Final Mortality Statistics, 1985," *Monthly Vital Statistics Report* (28 August 1987): 20.

of popularity in her school. However, through her sobbing and heartache, she told me she would trade it all for one more day of laughter with her brother.

We can look at all the statistics we want and still miss one of the most important facts about suicide. It is not a lone act. Suicide mars—even ruins—the lives of many, many people.

Linda Beahm, M.D.
Family Practice

> The Lord himself watches over you!
> The Lord stands beside you as your protective shade
> The sun will not hurt you by day nor the moon at night.
> The Lord keeps you from all evil
> and preserves your life.
> The Lord keeps watch over you as you come and go,
> both now and forever.
> *Psalm 121:5-8 (NIV)*

About the author

Donalyn is an inspirational writer and speaker. She has been an advocate for young people for many years. She lives in the foothills of the blue ridge mountains of Virginian with her horse friends, husband and four bird dogs.

Morgan James
Speakers Group

www.TheMorganJamesSpeakersGroup.com

We connect Morgan James published
authors with live and online events
and audiences whom will benefit
from their expertise.

 Morgan James makes all of our titles available
through the Library for All Charity Organization.

www.LibraryForAll.org

Printed in the USA
CPSIA information can be obtained
at www.ICGtesting.com
JSHW021956150824
68134JS00055B/1755